Life alert
1-800-6k4-2424

The Cradle of Texas

A Pictorial History of San Augustine County

Compiled and Edited by
Charla Jones

EAKIN PRESS ★ Austin, Texas

FIRST EDITION

Published in the United States of America
By Eakin Press
An Imprint of Sunbelt Media, Inc.
P. O. Drawer 90159 ★ Austin, TX 78709-0159

2 3 4 5 6 7 8 9

ISBN 1-57168-128-0

To my parents,
Charlie and Patsy,
and the people of San Augustine.
Without them, I would have never finished this project.

A war bond parade in downtown San Augustine around the time of W W I.
— Courtesy of San Augustine Public Library

Spectators stand along the sidewalks of San Augustine to watch the war bond parade.
— Courtesy of San Augustine Public Library

Contents

A sketch of the Mission Nuestra Señora de los Dolores de los Ais drawn by Raiford L. Stripling, a noted architect from San Augustine. The mission was said to have stood along the Ayish Bayou that runs through the town.

— Courtesy of Ray R. Stripling

Foreword

The town of San Augustine, Texas, San Augustine County, and the surrounding area has a deep, rich history. Numerous historians, not to mention the labor that went into George L. Crocket's epic work, *Two Centuries in East Texas,* have burned the midnight oil in compiling, chronicling, and composing the incredible events that gave birth and manhood to the Redlands of East Texas. How timely, and how fortunate we are that Charla Jones, a young Stephen F. Austin University graduate student in journalism, has joined the ranks of these illustrious historians with an engrossing pictorial history of San Augustine and San Augustine County.

Situated on the El Camino Real, the major link in the early 1800s between Spanish-governed Mexico and the westward moving frontier of the United States, San Augustine was laid out in 1833 by William McFarland and his son, Thomas S. McFarland. What better way to chronicle a segment of East Texas history, and the pioneers that lived that history, than a dramatic pictorial representation of a town from its birth in 1833 to the present, as it prepares to enter the twenty-first century.

The first time I was introduced to Charla Jones, I would have described her as an attractive young lady who was unassuming, a bit self-effacing, and extremely courteous. After I got to know her a little better, I added self-confidence, determination, perseverance, and a certain poise based in a faith of purpose. Later, as her "project" expanded far beyond its originally planned scope, I knew I was right about her perseverance, and added diligence, unrelenting and hard-working. I think Ms. Jones would agree that had it not been a "labor of love," her book would never have been finished. But then, over half of our storehouse of literature would never have been completed, except for the same reason. Thanks, Ms. Jones, for the "labor of love"!

Like most works of history, Ms. Jones' approach is chronological. She divides San Augustine's history into five major eras. She begins with Indian tribes and the Nuestra Senora de los Dolores de los Ais mission of the early eighteenth century and comes forward to the Battle of San Jacinto and Texas' independence. Next, she takes San Augustine through the days of the Republic, joining the United States as the twenty-eighth state, secession and the Civil War, reconstruction, and the end of the nineteenth century. The third section begins with the twentieth century, including the first railways into San Augustine, automobiles, World War I, and the beginning of the Great Depression (1929). The next-to-last section covers the Great Depression and World War II. The final segment begins in 1950 and moves through a "restoration period" to the present time.

Ms. Jones does this with over three hundred pictures strategically placed to distinguish and emphasize these five eras. Again, thanks, Charla Jones, for a remarkable pictorial tour of almost three hundred years of time travel through San Augustine's fantastic history.

Harry P. Noble, Jr.

Preface

I cannot say that I have ever been a serious student of historical studies. Like most people, I once thought that history is of the past and wondered why we should acknowledge it to move forward into the future.

As I researched my family tree in San Augustine, I noticed that there was no publication that showed the people and events of San Augustine. Stories, lectures, and essays have been written about the small redland town, but few photos or sketches could be found that showed the actuality of the people and the town from its early beginnings until now. I thought it was a shame that no one had, in one single publication, captured the life of San Augustine in picture form since it is one of the oldest and most important places in Texas.

I hope that this book will serve generations who want to see and not imagine what life in San Augustine was like. It serves my efforts well because it has allowed me a look into my family's past and the past of other San Augustine families as well.

Acknowledgments

Nothing is ever completely done by one individual. Without the help of the people of San Augustine, I would not have been able to compile this bit of history. They spent their time and energy to help me locate photographs, identify past and present citizens of San Augustine, and find information about the life of San Augustine and her citizens. It is my hope that the people of San Augustine will reap the benefits of this publication more than I will.

A project like this takes time and effort. I have spent many months in research to make this project a reality.

My parents have supported me through this project and often have chipped in to help when the research became too much for one person to handle. I hope they appreciate their daughter's work, and I thank them for being there for me when I needed their support.

Introduction

San Augustine is a gem in the history of Texas. A living portrait of the powerful history of Texas, it was from this small eastern town that men and women fought wars and wrote time-honored legislation that freed Texas from hostile governments and helped make it one of the fifty American states.

Ever since the first missionaries arrived in East Texas, people have traveled through San Augustine and marveled at her beauty. The colorful red dirt, thick lush forests, and warm southern climate of San Augustine convinced many settlers that it was a place to call home. The historical homes, markers, and sites which stand today offer images of what East Texas looked like to those settlers and weary travelers, many of whom are our ancestors.

Spanish missionaries first came to East Texas as early as 1690. They found the land inhabited by the Caddo Indians, who used the red land for farming and building hut homes. The Aies, a tribe from the nation of Caddo, was said to have lived along the banks of the Ayish Bayou which runs north and south through the west side of town. Along this bayou the Spanish missionaries erected missions, the most well-known being the Mission Nuestra Señora de los Dolores de los Ais, Our Lady of Sorrows. According to many sources, the missionaries apparently failed to truly convert all of the Indians to the Catholic religion, therefore causing the Spanish government to close the missions throughout East Texas.

The Spaniards often traded goods with the Indians and with the French who had controlled Louisiana. This made the town of San Augustine an important part of trade relations because it became the first town that travelers from Louisiana came to when traveling the El Camino Real, or the King's Road, into Mexico.

However, after Spain lost the Texas territory to Mexico, the Mission Nuestra Señora de los Dolores de los Ais was vacated and so was much of the San Augustine area. For the next several years, San Augustine would be inhabited and vacated almost four times before the Anglo-Saxon settlers with immense bravery established lifelong homes and businesses in the city. Mexican law struck fear in the settlers and so did the Indians. Tribes such as the Cherokees, who migrated into Texas, were often courted by the Mexican government to instill fear into the settlers and keep them from forming alliances against the Mexican government.

Even though the majority of the inhabitants in East Texas and San Augustine were Indians and missionaries during this time, historical records indicate that Anglo-Saxons were in the area too. According to these records, Richard Sims arrived in 1792, followed by Edmund Quirk, Nathan Davis, Jonas Harrison, and George English, the latter three settling near the Patroon Creek, northeast of San Augustine.

In his prolific book *Two Centuries in East Texas*, George Crocket described the Anglo-Saxon colonists who came to Texas in the early 1800s as farmers, businessmen, and lawyers. He believed that these people, the majority who came with Stephen F. Austin to Texas, possessed good educations and a depth of religious faith. They brought these qualities and built upon them in San Augustine in the form of schools and churches organized and built to serve the city in its educational and spiritual needs.

Historians tend to agree that San Augustine's golden days were during the era of the Republic of Texas. Prosperity boomed in the small town. Businessmen such as Matthew Cartwright and Stephen Blount and others opened retail stores for business. A. W. Canfield was the editor of *The Redlander,* one of the first newspapers in the Republic. Numerous cotton gins and lumber mills were built by people such as William Quirk, Wyatt Hanks, Donald McDonald, H. M. Hanks, John Sprowl and Alexander Horton, with Horatio Hanks having one of the best mills of its time along the banks of the Ayish Bayou.

According to George Crocket's account of East Texas, San Augustine was once considered the "Athens of Texas" because of its outstanding educational opportunities. One of the first known schools on record was a female academy located on the property where James P. Henderson would later build his home on South Liberty Street. As San Augustine grew, so did the small communities in the county. Each of these communities had a school and a church because transportation was limited for people to travel into the city to attend school and church services. Most of the rural schools lasted well into the 1930s and 1940s, when they finally closed due to transportation improvements and limited funds in rural areas.

San Augustine was home to two universities. The San Augustine University was incorporated on June 5, 1837. The citizens of San Augustine County who were on the board of trustees for the university were Elisha Roberts, Jesse Burditt, William McFarland, John Cartwright, Sumner Bacon, George Teal, Augustus Hotchkiss, Henry W. Augustine, Andrew J. Cunningham, Philip A. Sublett, Iredell D. Thomas, Albert Kellogg, Almanzon Huston, William Holman and Joseph Rowe. The Rev. Marcus Montrose, a Presbyterian minister, became the first president of the school. Its curriculum offered courses in English, mathematics, science, languages, and civics.

The Methodists of San Augustine also erected a university, which they named the Wesleyan College. Fourteen citizens including Francis Wilson, Littleton Fowler, Daniel Poe, and James P. Henderson served on the board of trustees. Unfortunately, both the Wesleyan College and San Augustine University closed their doors in 1847 as settlements outside of San Augustine began to offer educational opportunities.

The greatest lawyers of the Republic lived and practiced in San Augustine, including James P. Henderson and his partner, Thomas J. Rusk. Law and politics ruled the little town. Sam Houston even got into San Augustine politics. One of the requirements to own land or run for office under Mexican law was that a person had to show faith in the Catholic religion. Houston was therefore baptized a Catholic at the home of his friend Adolphus Sterne in Nacogdoches, with Mrs. Sterne serving as his godmother.

Many men would liberate and lead Texas during the 1830s. Alexander Horton fought in the Battle of San Jacinto. Stephen Blount and Edward O. Legrand were signers of the Texas Declaration of Independence. Kenneth L. Anderson served as vice-president of the Republic while James P. Henderson would be crowned the first governor of Texas. Oran M. Roberts also served as governor in later years. Other men, such as Thomas McFarland, Elisha Roberts, Ezekiel Cullen, and Alfred Polk, were just a few of San Augustine's citizens who served in the capacity of city, county, state, district, and federal offices.

Even though the Republic period was a time when women took a back seat to business and politics was considered to be only for men, one woman took exception to tradition. Although Frances Cox Henderson's role as First Lady of Texas allowed her opportunities to promote the betterment of San Augustine and Texas, it was her role as citizen, wife and mother that led her to do great things. She was solely responsible in obtaining the Episcopal faith for San Augustine. She saw a need for Episcopalian philosophy and called on the Episcopalians of Philadelphia, Pennsylvania, to send a missionary to San Augustine and serve the community. Because of her efforts, San Augustine was granted an Episcopalian church, Christ Church, led by the Rev. Henry Samson. His first duty as minister of Christ Church was to hold a funeral service for his oldest child, who died the day after his family arrived in San Augustine. The church has long since been a fixture in San Augustine, eventually providing historian George Crocket a pastoralship for nearly forty years. Mrs. Henderson, who was educated abroad, spoke six languages fluently and often entertained in the home she shared with James P. Henderson on what is now South Liberty Street.

What made San Augustine a bright star in the eyes of the Republic were the hundreds of people who, unknown or known, made San Augustine their home. These people came with desire and readiness to build homes, schools, churches, and businesses for the welfare of their community.

Churches were very important to the people of the Republic. When they left their original homes, they came to Texas with their individual faiths and made them part of San Augustine. Antioch Church of Christ, the oldest Church of Christ congregation in Texas, was established in 1833. Stephen Passmore donated to build a new church in 1880. Goodlaw's Presbyterian served the community west of San Augustine for many years. The First United Methodist Church was organized and later rebuilt on Liberty Street, thanks in part to the efforts of Methodist missionary Littleton Fowler, who was instrumental in building the first Protestant church in the state, McMahon's Chapel in Sabine County.

Today, San Augustine boasts more than twenty historic sites in the city and county, including many historic homes and markers of her most prominent citizens. William and Jacob Garrett, Matthew and Columbus Cartwright, Stephen Blount, the Hanks, Johnsons, and Teels, Ezekiel Cullen, Dr. B. F. Sharp, and many others built homes for their families that have been passed down through the generations to other families of San Augustine. These homes stand as San Augustine's testament that hard work by these families with a desire to make Texas home helped further the cause for her independence from Mexico.

San Augustine continued to prosper in the 1800s after Texas was inducted as a state of the United States. San Augustine, like many other southern cities, had to live through the trials and heartaches of the Civil War, which took many lives of its young citizens.

Most of those born between 1880 and 1900 lived to see the first ever telegraph, train, telephone and car in San Augustine. These inventions changed the face of San Augustine, but not the spirit of her citizens. With these inventions came new jobs, businesses, and trade with other cities. Also, these inventions made it easier for families and friends to correspond and travel.

Family names such as the Whittons, Johnsons, Crockets, Gambles, Harveys, Woods, and many others made up the roster of citizens living in San Augustine County. Smaller communities like Broaddus were prosperous, and places such as Bland Lake were thriving with lumber mills and cotton gins. Most communities within San Augustine County had gins, mills, lumber yards, churches, schools, and retail businesses. These businesses provided the people of each community jobs to support their families and gathering places for recreation. It was not unusual for people to have all that they needed in their communities without traveling into the city of San Augustine.

The onset of both WW I and WW II took again the lives of San Augustine's young men and women as they went abroad to fight against adversaries, as their ancestors had done during the Texas Revolution. San Augustine did its part in developing productive citizens to help the cause at home and abroad.

The communities all but disappeared with the beginning of the 1950s and beyond. Today, most communities which were once thriving little cities within themselves are now like ghost towns. However, the history of these communities that make up San Augustine County remains powerful because these communities gave birth to future leaders of the country and provided the older generations educations and recreation.

As one of the oldest towns in Texas, San Augustine has survived through prosperous years and torrential years. The people of San Augustine who came and laid the groundwork for Texas' independence and sought peace and justice are not forgotten by their descendants, who will now carry the torch for San Augustine and Texas into the twenty-first century.

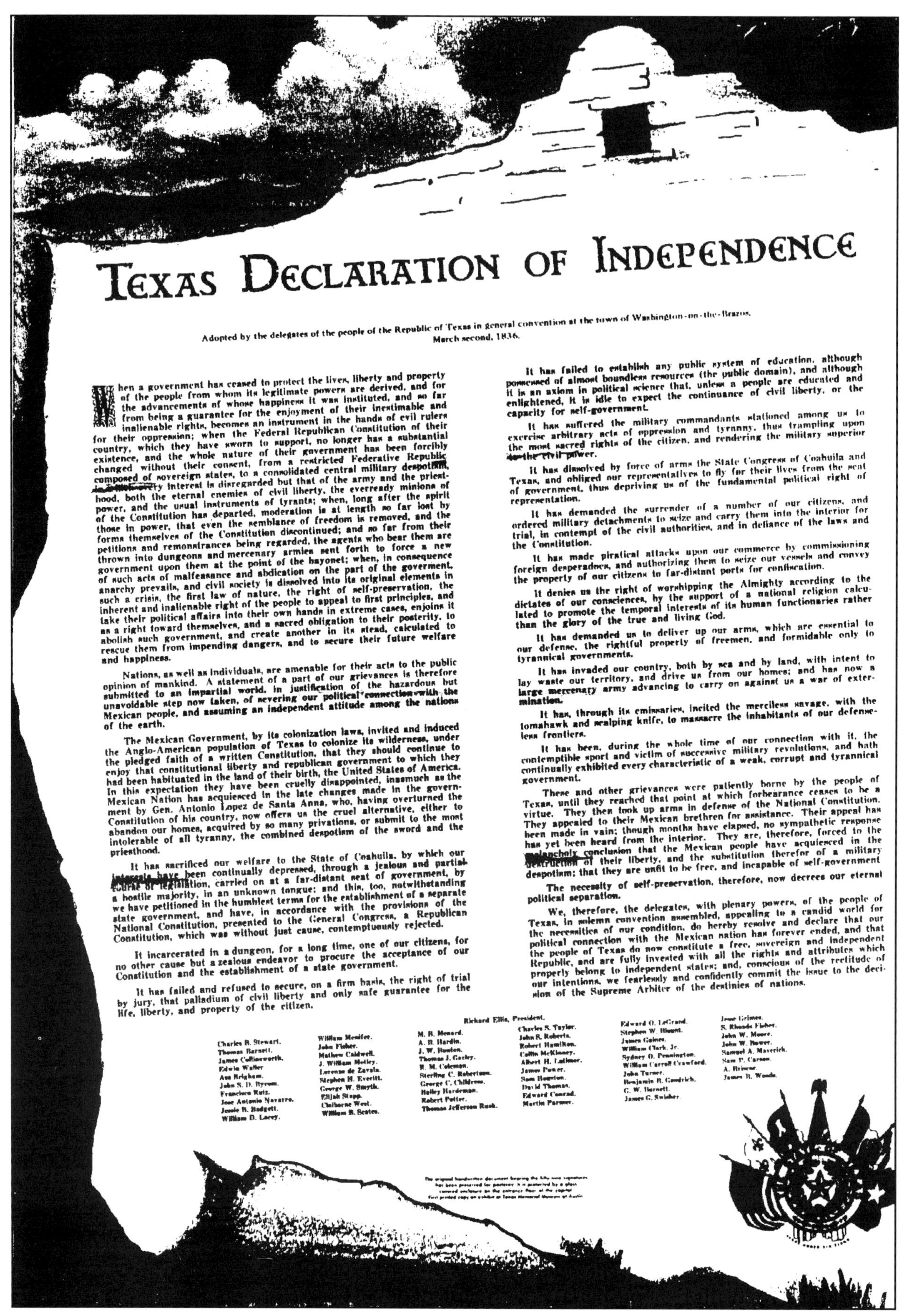

TEXAS DECLARATION OF INDEPENDENCE

Adopted by the delegates of the people of the Republic of Texas in general convention at the town of Washington-on-the-Brazos, March second, 1836.

When a government has ceased to protect the lives, liberty and property of the people from whom its legitimate powers are derived, and for the advancements of whose happiness it was instituted, and so far from being a guarantee for the enjoyment of their inestimable and inalienable rights, becomes an instrument in the hands of evil rulers for their oppression; when the Federal Republican Constitution of their country, which they have sworn to support, no longer has a substantial existence, and the whole nature of their government has been forcibly changed without their consent, from a restricted Federative Republic composed of sovereign states, to a consolidated central military despotism, [illegible]y interest is disregarded but that of the army and the priest-hood, both the eternal enemies of civil liberty, the everready minions of power, and the usual instruments of tyrants; when, long after the spirit of the Constitution has departed, moderation is at length so far lost by those in power, that even the semblance of freedom is removed, and the forms themselves of the Constitution discontinued; and so far from their petitions and remonstrances being regarded, the agents who bear them are thrown into dungeons and mercenary armies sent forth to force a new government upon them at the point of the bayonet; when, in consequence of such acts of malfeasance and abdication on the part of the goverment, anarchy prevails, and civil society is dissolved into its original elements in such a crisis, the first law of nature, the right of self-preservation, the inherent and inalienable right of the people to appeal to first principles, and take their political affairs into their own hands in extreme cases, enjoins it as a right toward themselves, and a sacred obligation to their posterity, to abolish such government, and create another in its stead, calculated to rescue them from impending dangers, and to secure their future welfare and happiness.

Nations, as well as individuals, are amenable for their acts to the public opinion of mankind. A statement of a part of our grievances is therefore submitted to an impartial world, in justification of the hazardous but unavoidable step now taken, of severing our political connection with the Mexican people, and assuming an independent attitude among the nations of the earth.

The Mexican Government, by its colonization laws, invited and induced the Anglo-American population of Texas to colonize its wilderness, under the pledged faith of a written Constitution, that they should continue to enjoy that constitutional liberty and republican government to which they had been habituated in the land of their birth, the United States of America. In this expectation they have been cruelly disappointed, inasmuch as the Mexican Nation has acquienced in the late changes made in the govern-ment by Gen. Antonio Lopez de Santa Anna, who, having overturned the Constitution of his country, now offers us the cruel alternative, either to abandon our homes, acquired by so many privations, or submit to the most intolerable of all tyranny, the combined despotism of the sword and the priesthood.

It has sacrificed our welfare to the State of Coahuila, by which our interests have been continually depressed, through a jealous and partial course of legislation, carried on at a far-distant seat of government, by a hostile majority, in an unknown tongue; and this, too, notwithstanding we have petitioned in the humblest terms for the establishment of a separate state government, and have, in accordance with the provisions of the National Constitution, presented to the General Congress, a Republican Constitution, which was without just cause, contemptuously rejected.

It incarcerated in a dungeon, for a long time, one of our citizens, for no other cause but a zealous endeavor to procure the acceptance of our Constitution and the establishment of a state government.

It has failed and refused to secure, on a firm basis, the right of trial by jury, that palladium of civil liberty and only safe guarantee for the life, liberty, and property of the citizen.

It has failed to establish any public system of education, although possessed of almost boundless resources (the public domain), and although it is an axiom in political science that, unless a people are educated and enlightened, it is idle to expect the continuance of civil liberty, or the capacity for self-government.

It has suffered the military commandants stationed among us to exercise arbitrary acts of oppression and tyranny, thus trampling upon the most sacred rights of the citizen, and rendering the military superior to the civil power.

It has dissolved by force of arms the State Congress of Coahuila and Texas, and obliged our representatives to fly for their lives from the seat of government, thus depriving us of the fundamental political right of representation.

It has demanded the surrender of a number of our citizens, and ordered military detachments to seize and carry them into the interior for trial, in contempt of the civil authorities, and in defiance of the laws and the Constitution.

It has made piratical attacks upon our commerce by commissioning foreign desperadoes, and authorizing them to seize our vessels and convey the property of our citizens to far-distant ports for confiscation.

It denies us the right of worshipping the Almighty according to the dictates of our consciences, by the support of a national religion calcu-lated to promote the temporal interests of its human functionaries rather than the glory of the true and living God.

It has demanded us to deliver up our arms, which are essential to our defense, the rightful property of freemen, and formidable only to tyrannical governments.

It has invaded our country, both by sea and by land, with intent to lay waste our territory, and drive us from our homes; and has now a large mercenary army advancing to carry on against us a war of exter-mination.

It has, through its emissaries, incited the merciless savage, with the tomahawk and scalping knife, to massacre the inhabitants of our defense-less frontiers.

It has been, during the whole time of our connection with it, the contemptible sport and victim of successive military revolutions, and hath continually exhibited every characteristic of a weak, corrupt and tyrannical government.

These and other grievances were patiently borne by the people of Texas, until they reached that point at which forbearance ceases to be a virtue. They then took up arms in defense of the National Constitution. They appealed to their Mexican brethren for assistance. Their appeal has been made in vain; though months have elapsed, no sympathetic response has yet been heard from the interior. They are, therefore, forced to the melancholy conclusion that the Mexican people have acquienced in the destruction of their liberty, and the substitution therefor of a military despotism; that they are unfit to be free, and incapable of self-government.

The necessity of self-preservation, therefore, now decrees our eternal political separation.

We, therefore, the delegates, with plenary powers, of the people of Texas, in solemn convention assembled, appealing to a candid world for the necessities of our condition, do hereby resolve and declare that our political connection with the Mexican nation has forever ended, and that the people of Texas do now constitute a free, sovereign and independent Republic, and are fully invested with all the rights and attributes which properly belong to independent states; and, conscious of the rectitude of our intentions, we fearlessly and confidently commit the issue to the deci-sion of the Supreme Arbiter of the destinies of nations.

Richard Ellis, President.

Charles B. Stewart.
Thomas Barnett.
James Collinsworth.
Edwin Waller
Asa Brigham.
John S. D. Byrom.
Francisco Ruiz.
Jose Antonio Navarro.
Jesse B. Badgett.
William D. Lacey.

William Menifee.
John Fisher.
Mathew Caldwell.
J. William Motley.
Lorenzo de Zavala.
Stephen H. Everitt.
George W. Smyth.
Elijah Stapp.
Claiborne West.
William B. Scates.

M. B. Menard.
A. B. Hardin.
J. W. Bunton.
Thomas J. Gazley.
R. M. Coleman.
Sterling C. Robertson.
George C. Childress.
Bailey Hardeman.
Robert Potter.
Thomas Jefferson Rusk.

Charles S. Taylor.
John S. Roberts.
Robert Hamilton.
Collin McKinney.
Albert H. Latimer.
James Power.
Sam Houston.
David Thomas.
Edward Conrad.
Martin Parmer.

Edward O. LeGrand.
Stephen W. Blount.
James Gaines.
William Clark, Jr.
Sydney O. Pennington.
William Carroll Crawford.
John Turner.
Benjamin B. Goodrich.
G. W. Barnett.
James G. Swisher.

Jesse Grimes.
S. Rhoads Fisher.
John W. Moore.
John W. Bower.
Samuel A. Maverick.
Sam P. Carson.
A. Briscoe.
James B. Woods.

Pioneers and the Republic

From its early beginning, the area that would become San Augustine was inhabited by several cultures including different Indian tribes, Spain, Mexico, and France; plus, the Anglo-Saxon and African-American emigrants who migrated from the east along the El Camino Real into the wilderness of Texas. These pioneers lived through harsh times before the Texas Revolution changed the physical and political boundaries of Texas and the struggling Republic finally achieved statehood as the twenty-eighth state of the United States.

Before the Revolution, the Ayish Bayou District consisted of San Augustine, its surrounding area, and parts of Shelby County. Most emigrants, on their way to a new life in a new land, traveled the King's Highway and stopped in San Augustine to rest. The hostility of the western Indians made the journey into the new territory frightening. Until Texas won its independence from Mexico, it was considered to be very hostile land. Even though the Aies Indians, who lived along the Ayish Bayou, were friendly, it was the western tribes that put fear into the emigrants' hearts. Mexico often made the situation worse by offering the tribes items if they helped keep the settlers from rebelling against the Mexican government.

The Caddoes were one of the main Indian tribes in East Texas, but they were not a feared as much as raiding tribes such as the Comanche and Apache. The Caddoes were genteel people who farmed the land and seldom bothered the settlers. The Caddo nation was divided into several hundred tribes, including the Aies tribes. Other local tribes were the Nacogdoches in Nacogdoches, Texas, and the Natchitoches on the Red River in Natchitoches, Louisiana. Dr. Donald E. Chipman, a history professor at North Texas, once wrote that the Spaniards considered the Caddoes to be the most desirable of Indians because of their highly productive system of agriculture. Research indicates that the Caddoes grew mostly corn, beans, sunflower seeds, squash, and tobacco. Although they were considered peaceful, they still carried on Indian traditions considered barbaric to the Spanish missionaries, and thus religious conversions often failed.

One of San Augustine's favorite sons, Alexander Horton, recalled how San Augustine looked when he and his mother first came to Texas: "I came to this county in 1824, found but few settlers and they were settled along the main road leading from Sabine to Nacogdoches. There was a small settlement down the Bayou of Mexicans and French that had settled there while was under the government of the king of Spain .... Early settlers of the county were high minded farmers who did not run here from crimes, but were honest industrious men who came here to better their condition being actuated by the large amount of land given to actual settlers, for they gave married men one league and single men one third of a league of land."

Not all men came to Texas for a better life. Some came to hide from the law. From 1806 until

1821, a strip of land called the Neutral Strip, or Lawless Strip, extended from Robeline, Louisiana, downward to the Sabine Lake and westward to Natchitoches in Louisiana. Criminals, outlaws, and other fugitives came to this area to avoid legal action against them for their crimes. This area was also called the "Free State of Sabine" because the area was not governed by any law or law officials during this time.

Horton recalled in his diary the first settlers of San Augustine: "The first house built in San Augustine was by R. C. McDaniel; the first store by I. D. Thomas, Sr. Then followed Matthew Cartwright and Augustus Hotchkiss: first tavern by A. Houston. Thus the town soon became considerable of a business place, and in 1834 San Augustine, Shelby and Sabine constituted one judicial district; John G. Love the first Presiding Judge, George English, Sheriff and the population increased considerably."

Stephen W. Blount and Edwin O. Legrand were two San Augustine pioneers who signed the Texas Declaration of Independence. Alexander Horton was aide-de-camp to Sam Houston when he and his Texas volunteers defeated the Mexican army during the Battle of San Jacinto. Mial Scurlock died at age twenty-five in the Alamo fighting for Texas' independence. Many others from San Augustine were chosen to take part in the politics of the Republic of Texas.

San Augustine lived under seven different flags during its early days. Not only was San Augustine once part of Spain, then Mexico, but also France, the Fredonians, the Republic of Texas, and the Confederate States, respectively, governed San Augustine. The seventh flag was the United States flag.

*St. Augustine Catholic Church is a result of the early Catholic missionaries' work in the San Augustine area. In 1847, the church was assigned a pastor, Rev. L.C.M. Chambodut, by the Diocese of Galveston. This facility is the only resemblance of the Catholic religion left in San Augustine after catholicism permeated the town during Mexico's reign over Texas. *Texas Historical Commission Marker*

— Charla Jones

A family crossing the Sabine River on the Gaines Ferry, c. 1930s. The wooden ferry resembles what James Gaines would have used when he helped migrants cross over the Sabine from Louisiana into Texas.

— Stephen F. Austin State University,
East Texas Research Center,
Karle Wilson Baker papers

The Jonas Harrison place on Patroon Creek, north of San Augustine. This picture was taken in the 1930s to show where the Harrison home site was formerly located. Harrison worked tirelessly for Texas' independence before his death in 1836.

— Stephen F. Austin State University,
East Texas Research Center,
Karle Wilson Baker papers

*Texas Historical Marker honoring Kenneth L. Anderson, the last vice-president of the Republic of Texas. He was an outstanding orator and debater as well as a law partner with Thomas J. Rusk and James P. Henderson. *Texas Historical Commission Marker*

— Charla Jones

*The Antioch Church of Christ was organized in 1833 by William P. Defee. In 1870, a building was constructed for the church on land that belonged to Stephen Passmore. The current building was completed in 1938. *Texas Historical Commission Marker*

— Patsy Jones

*Col. Philip A. Sublett (1802-1850) was a pioneer who served as a delegate to the conventions in 1832-33 and in the capture of San Antonio in 1835. Sublett and most of his descendants are interred on the Sublett ranch just east of San Augustine. *Texas Historical Commission Marker*

— Charla Jones

The home of Thomas McFarland, the son of William McFarland. Both came to Texas in 1830. In 1833, Thomas McFarland laid out the town of San Augustine on land he purchased from Chichester Chaplin. Thomas McFarland served in the senate and as chief justice of San Augustine County.

— Stephen F. Austin State University,
East Texas Research Center

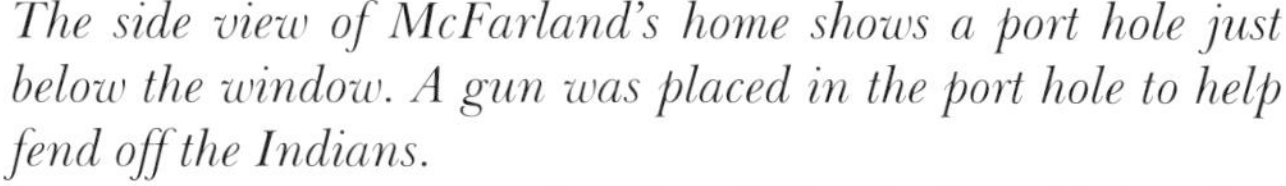

The side view of McFarland's home shows a port hole just below the window. A gun was placed in the port hole to help fend off the Indians.

— Stephen F. Austin State University,
East Texas Research Center

This photograph is of a painting of Alexander Horton handing Sam Houston a horse during the Battle of San Jacinto. The painting hangs in the Texas Senate chamber. The photograph was taken by Richard Murphy, a descendant of Horton.

— Painting by McArdle; photograph by Richard Murphy

Col. Stephen W. Blount and Mary Blount, his wife. Blount was a signer of the Texas Declaration of Independence. He was also a delegate to the Convention of 1836 and the first county clerk of San Augustine.

— Stephen F. Austin State University, East Texas Research Center

Judge William B. Ochiltree, who came to Texas in 1839. In 1842, he became district judge of the Fifth District. He also served Texas as secretary of the treasury in Anson Jones' cabinet, attorney general in 1845, and as a member of the Secession Convention in 1861.

— Red Land Masonic Lodge, San Augustine

John A. Greer was an early settler in Ironosa. He came to Texas in 1837. He was appointed and elected to many offices including president of the senate in the Sixth, Seventh, Eighth, and Ninth Congresses, secretary of the treasury upon Ochiltree's resignation, and lieutenant governor thrice.

— Red Land Masonic Lodge, San Augustine

Franklin B. Sexton came to Texas at a young age. He graduated from San Augustine's Wesleyan College in 1846 and became a law partner with Ezekiel Cullen. He would later be elected to the House of Representatives of the Congress of the Confederacy.

— Red Land Masonic Lodge, San Augustine

J.C. Rohte was an early parishioner of the Christ Church. There is little written about Rohte other than he supported the Episcopalian faith in San Augustine.

— Red Land Masonic Lodge, San Augustine

Nicholas H. Darnell came to Texas from Tennessee. He was elected to the Seventh Congress and Speaker of the House. He was presumed to have won the position of the first lieutenant governor, but lost that position when the ballots were recounted.

— Red Land Masonic Lodge, San Augustine

Travis Broocks arrived in Texas in 1838 with his wife and children. He was given the title of general during the war between the Regulators and Moderators in 1844. He purchased Elisha Roberts' home site and lived there until he died.

— Red Land Masonic Lodge, San Augustine

Ezekiel Cullen came to Texas from Georgia in 1835. He practiced law in San Augustine from 1837 to 1848. He also served as a member of the Third Congress of the Texas Republic and as a representative. He also became judge of the First Judicial District and associate justice of the Supreme Court of the Republic of Texas and purser of the U.S. Navy. This photograph of Cullen hangs above the fireplace in the front parlor of the Cullen House in San Augustine.

— Ezekiel Cullen House Museum, San Augustine

*Chinagrove was owned by Dr. B.F. Sharp, son of M.D.L. Sharp, who settled in San Augustine around 1848. He bought Chinagrove from S.S. Davis, a former volunteer of the Texas Revolution, a representative, and sheriff of San Augustine County. Sharp's wife, Martha Ann Hall, renamed the place Chinagrove because of the number of china trees that were on the land. *Historical Medallion Home*

— Charla Jones

*The Polk Home was originally built in 1840 for Ransom H. Horn by Horn and his brother F.N. Horn. Harry K. Polk, a grandson to Judge Alfred Polk, bought the home. *Historical Medallion Home*

— Patsy Jones

*A marker commemorating the site of Elisha Roberts' home. Roberts came to Texas in 1824 and served as alcalde in 1831. He also served on the board of trustees of the San Augustine University. *Texas Historical Commission Marker*

— Patsy Jones

This picture of a M.E. Church was taken from a postcard owned by Anne Miller Wharton's mother. The picture of the church resembles sketches of the original First United Methodist Church on Main Street. The writing below the picture indicates the church was built in 1839.

— Courtesy of Anne Miller Wharton

*The Jerusalem Memorial Christian Methodist Episcopal Church is considered one of the oldest black congregations in the state. It was organized around 1845 after two slaves, Sutton and Bartlett, were granted licenses to preach in what was called the church on the branch. It later became the Christian Methodist Episcopal Church in 1954. *Texas Historical Commission Marker*

— Charla Jones

*The Wade House or "Hospitality House" was built around 1837, when Thomas Sebastian Cabot Wade moved to Texas and settled on FM 705 outside of San Augustine. Wade was a half-brother to E.O. Legrand and worked in San Augustine as a farmer, a gin and grist mill operator, and owner of a mercantile store which was located across from the home. *Historical Medallion Home*

— Charla Jones

Sam Houston was almost a native son of San Augustine. He had many friends in the town, including James P. Henderson and Thomas J. Rusk, whom Houston and his wife occasionally visited.

— Courtesy of the Citizens of San Augustine; reprinted

These sketches represent the San Augustine University and the old Masonic Lodge. However, there has been much debate as to which building is which and if one building housed the Wesleyan University.

— Stephen F. Austin State University,
East Texas Research Center,
George Crocket Sketches of
San Augustine and Nacogdoches

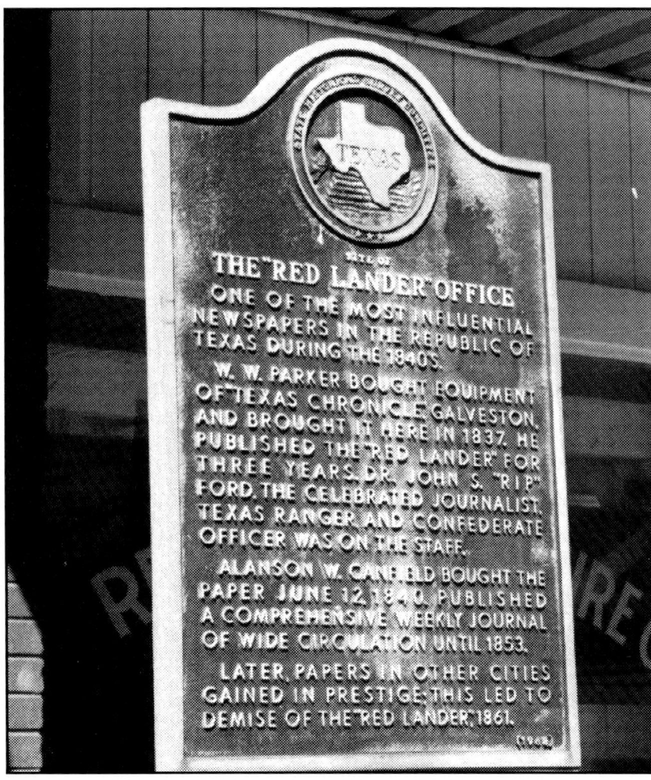

The Redlander *was first printed in 1837 and later bought by A.W. Canfield, who operated the influential newspaper during the Republic until 1853. The newspaper office was located on Columbia Street across from where Nelsyn's is located today. *Texas Historical Commission Marker*

— Charla Jones

William Prather Harvey, left, and Stephen Prather Harvey, great-grandfather of Juanice Harvey Beard. These brothers were the sons of Blassingame W. Harvey. Stephen, born 1829, married Frances Ann Hill in 1850.

— Courtesy of Juanice Harvey Beard

Blassingame W. Harvey (1792-1867). He was born in North Carolina. He was married to his third wife, Eliza Mary Ann Prather, in 1826. He is the great-great-grandfather of Juanice Harvey Beard.

— Courtesy of Juanice Harvey Beard

Stephen Prather, the father of Eliza Mary Ann Prather and great-great-great-grandfather of Juanice Harvey Beard, c. early 1800s.

— Courtesy of Juanice Harvey Beard

*Edward O. Legrand came to Texas and served in the San Jacinto battle, but his most famous contribution to Texas was as signer of the Texas Declaration of Independence. *Texas Historical Commission Marker*

— Charla Jones

*The Milton Garrett home on Hwy. 21 west of San Augustine. This hand-hewn log home is one of the oldest homes in San Augustine, built in 1826. Milton was the brother of William Garret and son of Jacob Garret. Architect Raiford Stripling restored and lived in the home. *Historical Medallion Home*

— Charla Jones

A sketch by George Crocket of the businesses in San Augustine including those of Matthew Cartwright, Brown and Burrus, and Jackson and Arnold.

— Stephen F. Austin State University, East Texas Research Center, George Crocket Sketches of San Augustine and Nacogdoches

*Col. Stephen Blount residence on Columbia Street was built by Augustus Phelps in 1839. Blount and his wife, Mary, lived in the home along with their children. Raiford Stripling restored the home. *Historical Medallion Home*

— Charla Jones

*The Columbus Cartwright home was built in 1838. Raiford Stripling restored the home. *Historical Medallion Home*

— Patsy Jones

*The Cullen House was built by Augustus Phelps in 1839. Ezekiel Cullen and his family lived in the home for many years. In 1952, Cullen's grandson, Hugh Roy Cullen, donated the home to the Daughters of the Republic of Texas. *Historical Medallion Home*

— Charla Jones

*The home of Texas pioneer Col. Philip A. Sublett. It is east of San Augustine and not far from where Sublett's father-in-law, Elisha Roberts, lived. *Historical Medallion Home*

— Charla Jones

A sketch by George Crocket of the Almanson Huston-James Anderson-C. C. Johnson home.

— Stephen F. Austin State University, East Texas Research Center, George Crocket Sketches of San Augustine and Nacogdoches

James Pinckney Henderson, former lawyer of San Augustine and first governor of the state of Texas. Henderson was an accomplished student of law and politics and served Texas well.

— Stephen F. Austin State University, East Texas Research Center

Thomas J. Rusk was known mostly for his work in Nacogdoches. However, he was a law partner of James P. Henderson in San Augustine.

— Stephen F. Austin State University, East Texas Research Center

*The Memorial Presbyterian Church was first organized at Goodlaw's Schoolhouse, four miles west of the town in 1838 by the Rev. Hugh Wilson, D.D. Some of the present members are descendants of the twenty-two charter members. In 1840, the congregation moved to San Augustine and renamed it the Memorial Presbyterian Church. The sanctuary has a "boat shaped" ceiling, a reflection of its builder, shipbuilder A.C. Ketchum. *Texas Historical Commission Marker*

— Charla Jones and Patsy Jones

Matthew Cartwright and his wife, Amanda Holman Cartwright, lived in San Augustine with their family. Matthew was a well-known businessman in San Augustine.

— Courtesy of Anna V. Cartwright

*The Matthew Cartwright home, built for Isaac Campbell by Augustus Phelps in 1839. Cartwright bought the home in 1847 for his wife, Amanda, and their family. *Historical Medallion Home*

— Patsy Jones

A sketch of the Canfield House by George Crocket.

— Stephen F. Austin State University,
East Texas Research Center,
George Crocket Sketches of San Augustine and Nacogdoches

A sketch of the Alexander Horton place by George Crocket.

— Stephen F. Austin University,
East Texas Research Center,
George Crocket Sketches of San Augustine and Nacogdoches

*Christ Church was organized in 1838 due to the tremendous efforts of Frances Cox Henderson. The original church was built in 1851, but later destroyed by a storm in 1859. In 1870, the present building was constructed. The Rev. George Crocket served as rector for over forty years. *Texas Historical Commission Marker*

— Charla Jones

William Washington Whitton (1823-1915) and Mary Lydia Hughes (1824-1905). The Whittons came to Texas from Georgia in 1851, settling in San Augustine County in 1855. Their children were William Newton, Mary Comal (Baker), Caroline Matilda (Baggett), John Jasper, James Benjamin, Andrew Jackson, Nancy E. (Billingsley), Pinkney Henderson, Jefferson Davis, Millie Frances (Willard), and Columbus Lee.

— Courtesy of Dr. J.M. and McXie Whitton Martin

John Gaston Baggett (1820-1886) and his wife, Mary Elizabeth Armstrong (1827-1917). They moved to San Augustine from Georgia in 1873, along with their nine children: William Jefferson, Thomas Wesley Moore, James Aberick, John Mack Henry, Lavinia Catherine (Eppes), Micajah, Andrew Gaston, Sarah Jane (Eppes), and Martha Ann (Bland).

— Courtesy of Dr. J.M. and McXie Whitton Martin

James A. Robinson (1836-1911) and his wife, Mary Smith Robinson (1849-1899), were the parents of Amanda Robinson Mathews.

— Courtesy of Woodrow Mathews

Inlow Mathews (1813-1879). He came to Texas with his brother in 1849. Inlow and Jeannett were the parents of Inlow Lee Mathews and the grandparents of J.P., Mary, and Woodrow Mathews.

— Courtesy of Woodrow Mathews

Marcus Lafayette Sharp, M.D. (1789-1862). He served in the War of 1812 and in the Indian Wars with General Jackson.

— Stephen F. Austin State University, East Texas Research Center, Mattie Sharp Brewer papers

Jeannett Hoffman Mathews (1826-1897), the wife of Inlow Mathews.

— Courtesy of Woodrow Mathews

Frances Cox Henderson, wife of James Pinckney Henderson and former First Lady of Texas.
— Courtesy of Christ Church Episcopal, San Augustine

James Pinckney Henderson, the first governor of Texas.
— Courtesy of Christ Church Episcopal, San Augustine

Capt. William Scurlock, a brother to Mial Scurlock who was killed in the Alamo.
—Courtesy of Essie Martin: printed in *The Scurlocks: Seekers of Freedom*

Statehood: A New Beginning for Texas

The United States Congress and President James Polk in December 1845 approved the constitution to annex Texas. In February of 1846, President Anson Jones relinquished his authority to James Pinckney Henderson, the new governor of Texas. Jones stated, "The final act in this great drama is now performed. The Republic of Texas is no more."

Although the people continued to migrate to Texas during and after the Revolution, San Augustine was still a frontier town. The roads, public officials, and court system were not as well developed as were the towns from which the emigrants came. William R. Hogan once said San Augustine was the one town in the Republic of Texas to be far ahead of the rest of Texas towns in civilization and culture: ". . . in the early eighteen-forties San Augustine had been notable not only for two praiseworthy educational ventures, but also for the high cultural level of many of its citizens. Indeed, San Augustine of that day must provide the best in the civilization of the period. Even now, a century later, something of the atmosphere of good taste still lingers in the fine clear-cut lines of its old homes."

Family, education, and religion were most important to the settlers of San Augustine, and it is evident in the number of schools and churches which were built after the Revolution. A few of the churches, thanks in part to its members, are still standing. Among these churches are two begun by African-American congregations. A story of Roberts Baptist Church was written in 1972 by Joanna Phillips, a great-great-granddaughter of an original congregational member, Liza Roberts. Roberts Baptist Church was built on land given by Elisha Roberts. The Jerusalem Memorial Christian Methodist Episcopal Church congregation was founded by two slaves, Sutton and Bartlett, around 1845, and the continuing work of this church body makes it one of the oldest African-American churches in Texas.

In the mid-1800s, San Augustine bustled with business activities. Many of the citizens were beginning to live what has been called the American Dream. In 1860, a list of San Augustine's wealthiest people were Matthew Cartwright, Calloway Deen, William Garrett, Iredell D. Thomas, and Richard Waterhouse. These men were engaged in agriculture, land speculation, and retail. Others ran successful businesses with cotton gins, lumber mills, the practice of law, and politics.

Many of the heroes of Texas' independence and its annexation into the United States came from San Augustine and the surrounding East Texas area. It was not uncommon for Texas' most famous icon, Sam Houston, to linger in San Augustine visiting his good friends, such as Iredell D. Thomas and Philip Sublett.

San Augustine was home to two of Texas' governors during the 1800s. James Pinckney Henderson was the first governor of Texas from 1846 to 1847. Had Kenneth L. Anderson not died on his way home to San Augustine, he instead of Henderson would have been governor.

Henderson and his wife, Frances Cox Henderson, lived on South Liberty Street and attended Christ Church Episcopal in San Augustine. Henderson, a native of North Carolina, was said to have been the best orator of his time. His education from Pleasant Retreat Academy and Chapel Hill College, two well-noted educational institutions in North Carolina, served him well as a lawyer and statesman. He practiced law in San Augustine with Kenneth L. Anderson and his good friend, Thomas J. Rusk. In 1857, after Rusk committed suicide, the Seventh Texas Legislature elected Henderson to fill the vacancy in the U.S. Senate that his long-time friend and partner had left.

Oran Milo Roberts was another governor from San Augustine, who served from 1879 to 1883. His milestone while in office was the building of the State Capitol in Austin. Roberts was a well-educated man originally from Alabama. After coming to Texas, he was a faculty member of the University of San Augustine. He later led an infantry regiment during the Civil War.

Despite his downsizing of funds to reduce the state debt, Roberts made major improvements in Texas' higher education system while in office. He helped found Sam Houston State and Prairie View and helped to create the University of Texas, which started classes in 1883. After Roberts served his second gubernatorial term, he taught law at the University of Texas and helped create the Texas State Historical Association.

Roberts made San Augustine famous in 1893 in a lecture he gave at the University of Texas. He accented the important contributions that the small Texas town made in the Revolution and the reshaping of Texas after the defeat of Mexico. He lauded the men who gave of their time and lives to the cause of Texas and emphasized how their actions should never be forgotten.

Former U. S. Ambassador to Australia Edward A. Clark once told of an anecdote of Governor Roberts. "Someone told Gov. Roberts that Texas was 'going to hell.' Gov. Roberts then stated: 'I don't know about that, but I assure you that if it does, it will be according to law!'"

In O. M. Roberts' Writings and Acts was found the marriage ceremony of Alexander Horton and Mary Harrol on December 30, 1847. Assuming that Roberts conducted the ceremony, the words in which he spoke indicate quite a different style than today's language. After the Hortons said "I do," Roberts then replied: "May the Texas plume expand its beauty and despense its fragrance beneath the fostering shade of the oak of San Jacinto. May connubial bliss cement this nuptial tie and may heaven's richest blessings crown the union. . ."

The Civil War would become another major crisis for the people of San Augustine. As with other Southern states, Texas ceded from the United States and sons and daughters from San Augustine were once again sent to defend Texas. Nine of San Augustine's Confederate soldiers are interred in the Antioch Cemetery along with some of the original members of the Antioch Church of Christ. Dr. Isiah Jackson Roberts was one of those who gave of their time and expertise to the soldiers of the Civil War. Dr. Roberts worked as a surgeon for those wounded in action.

The author's grandmother once said she could remember her grandparents, John and Cynthia Leach Dwire, burning their Confederate money in the backyard after the war ended. Since Texas had been a Confederate state and therefore used the Confederate currency, people had to either burn or otherwise destroy the useless money at war's end.

*Hillcrest was built in 1872 by William B. Leonard. He sold the home to Matthew Cartwright's son, Leonidas, who had it enlarged in 1878. *Historical Medallion Home*

— Charla Jones

*The Lafayette "Pet" Sharp home was built in the 1850s by W.H. Horn and F.N. Horn. Sharp bought the home in 1884. *Historical Medallion Home*

— Charla Jones

*The Old Union School building, which still stands outside of San Augustine in the Denning community, 1277 FM. Ex-students erected a memorial in tribute to Amanda Smith Matthews who taught at Union from 1889 to 1934, and to Columbus Horn, who donated the land and assisted in the building of the school. *Texas Historical Commission Marker*

— Charla Jones

*The William Garrett plantation was built in 1861. Garrett, the son of Jacob Garrett, supposedly built the home "patterned after his homesick daughter's dream." *Historical Medallion Home*

— Charla Jones

*The Herring home, or Straddlefork, was erected in 1875 for Jacob Herring, who came to Texas in 1836. Former Ambassador to Australia Edward Clark and his wife, Anne, purchased the home in 1965. *Historical Medallion Home*

— Charla Jones

*Roberts Baptist Church was founded by the Rev. John Patton in 1872. The original church was built on land given by Elisha Roberts, but was moved to its present site on South Liberty in 1918. Some of its present members are descendants of the original members of the church and have been faithful to the church for generations. *Texas Historical Commission Marker*

— Charla Jones

*The First United Methodist Church was later rebuilt on Liberty Street in 1897 on land donated by Columbus Cartwright. The church is one of the oldest Protestant congregations in Texas. *Texas Historical Commission Marker*

— Charla Jones

*McRae Presbyterian Church was built in 1882. It was named after Rev. D. A. McRae. Capt. T. W. Blount's fieldhands cut the lumber used to build the church. The McRae cemetery next to the church is where Rev. McRae was buried after he had served the McRae congregation for forty years. *Texas Historical Commission Marker*

— Charla Jones

Matthew and Amanda Cartwright's son, Columbus, and his wife, Sally Cartwright.

— Courtesy of Anna V. Cartwright

Seated are Cynthia Leach Dwire and her husband, John Dwire. Standing behind them is their son, Benjamin Franklin Dwire, the great-grandfather of Charla Jones.

— Courtesy of E. W. Campbell family

The Bland Mill on Bland Lake. Bland Lake, built around 1894 or 1895 by James Jefferson Bland, was originally used to operate a cotton gin and grist mill. About 1921, Bland Lake became a recreational spot for swimming, picnicking, boating, and dancing on the pavilion.

— Courtesy of Sallie Richards Whitton

W.K. (Bud) Knight, Agnes Williams Sparks' maternal grandfather. His wife was Julia Tinsley Knight.

— Courtesy of Agnes Williams Sparks

James Benjamin Whitton (1853-1946) and Ida Lavinia Baggett (1870-1947), possibly on their wedding day. She is wearing her wedding outfit. Their children were Thomas Lee, William Newt, Irene, Abbie King, Nugent, Jesse Benjamin, Hattie Nancy, Julian, and Lillis.

—Coutesy of Dr. J. M. and McXie Whitton Martin

*The Hollis building was built in the 1800s and was the location of Kenneth L. Anderson's office. *Texas Historical Marker*

— Charla Jones

Agnes W. Sparks' grandmother, Susan Virginia Murphy Williams.

— Courtesy of Agnes Williams Sparks

William E. Williams, Agnes W. Sparks' paternal grandfather. He was married to Susan Virginia Murphy Williams.

— Courtesy of Agnes Williams Sparks

Brune Wall, father of an early San Augustine sheriff.
— Courtesy of Agnes Williams Sparks

Fannie Burns Baldree.
— Courtesy of Agnes Williams Sparks

William Kendall, grandfather of Bud Knight. Mr. Kendall served as a surgeon in the Civil War.
— Courtesy of Agnes Williams Sparks

Nancy Armour, great-grandmother of Mamie Ruth Patterson. She was married to Tucker Greer.
— Courtesy of Mamie Ruth Patterson

The home of Stephen Prather Harvey, son of Blassingame W. Harvey on Harvey Creek. The home was built around 1850. In the picture are Glenn Harvey, Sallie Wise Harvey, Lucy Harvey, Comunchie Harvey, Skillern Harvey, and Sallie Harvey. Photo printed in Huntington-Zavalla Gazette.
— Courtesy of Juanice Harvey Beard; printed in *Huntington-Zavalla Gazette*, 1976

The Rawson family, from left to right seated: Thomas Lewis Rawson and William B. Rawson. Standing left to right: Robert R. Rawson, Warren Harp Rawson, and Edwin Lee (Bud) Rawson. Harp Rawson was Lester Rawson's father.
— Courtesy of Rosine Sanders Rawson

Pinkney Henderson Whitton.
— Courtesy of Rosa Lee Whitton Ambrose

Nannie Lane was 101 when this picture was taken in 1978. She died at age 103. She was the mother of William Lane and mother-in-law to Gertrude Johnson Lane.
— Courtesy of William and Gertrude Johnson Lane; printed in *San Augustine Tribune,* 1980

Nancy McEver Polk, Anne Miller Wharton's great-great-great-grandmother.
— Courtesy of Anne Miller Wharton

Robena West Miller (1857-1942) and Lee Roy Miller (1855-1925). They had seven children including John Bennett Miller, Anne Miller Wharton's grandfather.
— Courtesy of Anne Miller Wharton

Samuel Willard and Nancy Allgood Willard. They were the parents of Nannie Willard Whitton and the maternal grandparents of Rosa Whitton Ambrose, Harlowe Whitton Johnson, Allene Whitton Hankla, and Mildred Whitton Smith.
— Courtesy of Rosa Lee Whitton Ambrose

Sarah Isabell Polk Smith, Anne Miller Wharton's great-great- grandmother and daughter to Nancy McEver Polk.
— Courtesy of Anne Miller Wharton

Left to right are Ella Sharp Walding and her parents Elza Teel Sharp (b. 1832) and Dr. James Henry Sharp (b. 1816), c. 1885. The Sharps were Val Sharp's great-grandparents.
— Courtesy of Val and Lucy Sharp

Inlow Lee Mathews (1864-1932), one of nine children to Inlow and Jeannett Hoffman Mathews.
— Courtesy of Woodrow Mathews

Amanda Robinson Mathews. She married Inlow Lee Mathews in 1908.
— Courtesy of Woodrow Mathews

Gertrude Johnson Lane's parents, Dan and Mary D. Johnson, both born in 1893.
— Courtesy of Gertrude Johnson Lane

Sam and Mary Passmore.
— Courtesy of Marlon and Brownie Joe Minton

George Washington Brewer, great-grandfather to Liz Brewer Ware.
— Courtesy of Leeon and Liz Brewer Ware

Henderson Berry and his wife, Emma. Emma was a sister to Leeon Ware's mother, Caddie Richey Ware. Henderson Berry was a grandfather to Helen Beasley and great-grandfather of Mike Beasley.
— Courtesy of Leeon and Liz Brewer Ware

Miss Hattie Collins (Mrs. George Slaughter) of San Augustine.
— Stephen F. Austin State University, East Texas Research Center, Mattie Sharp Brewer papers

George Crocket's home across from the Christ Church.
— Stephen F. Austin State University, East Texas Research Center, Karle Wilson Baker papers

The sisters of George Crocket.
— Stephen F. Austin State University, East Texas Research Center, Mattie Sharp Brewer papers

Mariah Josephine McCauley Gamble and her husband, Hugh Lawson Gamble, in around 1895. These photos were made from tintype pictures found in the old trunk of their son, Sam Gamble.
— Courtesy of Verline Gamble Stewart

Dr. Benjamin Franklin Sharp.
— Stephen F. Austin State University, East Texas Research Center, Mattie Sharp Brewer papers

Georgia Mae Woods Mathews' father, George Washington Woods, b. 1882, right, and his brother, Columbus Woods.
— Courtesy of Georgia Mae Woods Mathews

George Louis Crocket, father of George Crocket.
— Stephen F. Austin State University, East Texas Research Center, Mattie Sharp Brewer papers

William Ponder's sons from left to right front row are John, Jeff, Thad, and Monroe. Back row includes Houston (Lena Ponder Arnold's father) and Berry (Winnie Ponder Nance's father).
— Courtesy of Jim and Winnie Ponder Nance

The home place on Ponder Lane at Bland Lake. Seated in front are Angelina Roberts Ponder and William Farrar Ponder. Seated on the fence is John Ponder and on the ground in front is Lon Ware. Others include Cortie and Julie Roberts, Mary Ponder Hasley, Birdie Hasley, Cal Hasley, Jim and Sam Roberts, Joe Roberts, Martha "Matt" Ponder Roberts, who is holding Bertha, and on the fence is Thad Ponder, behind William. William Ponder was a Civil War veteran. He and his wife, Angelina, were the grandparents of Winnie Ponder Nance.

— Courtesy of Jim and Winnie Ponder Nance

Simon Peter Burkett.

— Courtesy of San Augustine Public Library

Christina Burkett Lacy, mother of Simon Burkett. She was a Seminole Indian from Florida.

— Courtesy of San Augustine Public Library

A sketch of the San Augustine Public School (1875-1905) drawn by George Crocket.

— Stephen F. Austin University, East Texas Research Center, George Crocket Sketches of San Augustine

John W. Newton, Robert Newton's father. John Newton was a Civil War veteran.

— Courtesy of Alvin Newton

William Washington Whitton as an older man. He was the grandfather of Rosa Whitton Ambrose, Harlowe Whitton Johnson, and Allene Whitton Hankla.

— Courtesy of Rosa Lee Whitton Ambrose

James A. (Bud) Langford and his wife, Zida Omega McRae Langford, Mary Ben Hensarling's great-grandparents.

— Courtesy of Mary Ben Hensarling

John Thomson, Sr., front row and center, with his sons. From left to right, front row: Ray and Dewitt. Back row includes John, Elec, and Fred. John Thomson, Sr. was Mamie Ware Taylor's grandfather.

— Courtesy of Mamie Ware Taylor

John Taylor, father of Dock Taylor and great-grandfather of Belinda Taylor Coulter. Liberty Hill Baptist Church was built on land he gave to the church.
— Courtesy of Audrey Taylor

William Washington Watson and his wife, Nancy Narcissus Byrd Watson.
— Courtesy of Sandra Bennett

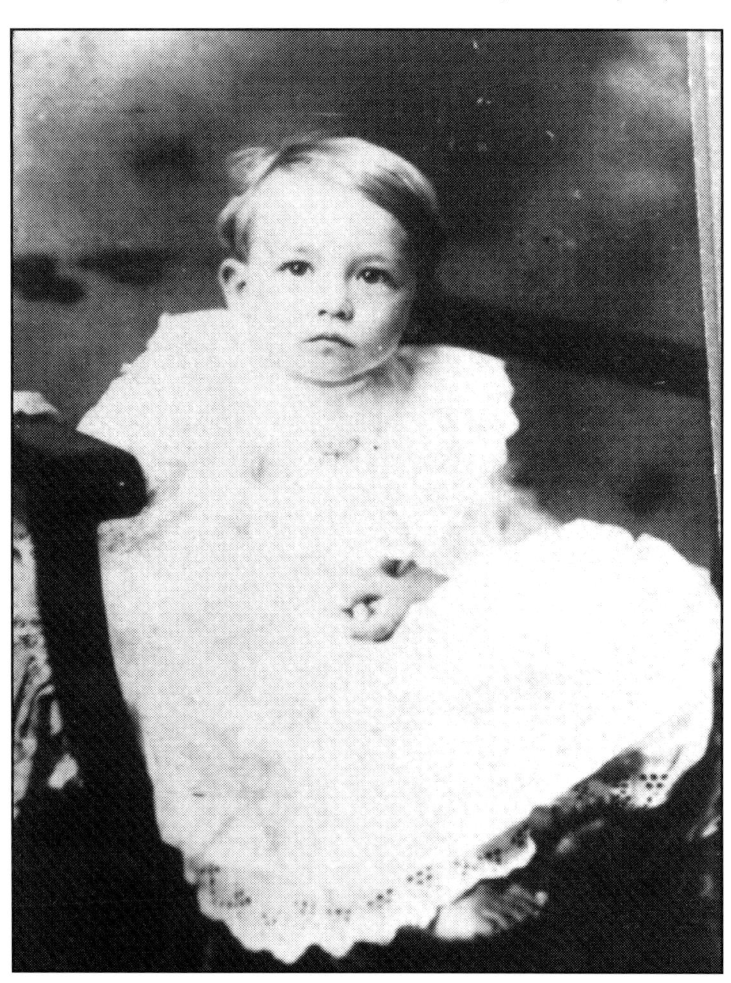

Elbert Haley.
— Courtesy of Sandra Bennett

Dr. Isiah Jackson Roberts was an early physician in San Augustine. According to George Crocket's account of San Augustine, Dr. Roberts was a well-known surgeon in East Texas, with patients from all over coming to see him for treatment. He also served as a surgeon in the Civil War.
— Courtesy Red Land Masonic Lodge, San Augustine

Charleton Payne came to Texas from Mississippi. He was a lawyer and business partner of George F. Crocket. He also served on the bench of the Fifth District and as a district judge.
— Courtesy of Red Land Masonic Lodge, San Augustine

Rufus Price came to Texas from Tennessee and practiced law in San Augustine for many years. He was appointed as district judge and worked and was friends with Franklin B. Sexton, Samuel B. Bewley, and William W. Wallace.
— Courtesy of Red Land Masonic Lodge, San Augustine

An oil painting of Iredell D. Thomas, grandfather of Seymour Thomas, who painted this portrait.
— Charla Jones, Ezekiel Cullen House and Museum, San Augustine

James Jefferson Bland (1861-1940) and his wife, Martha (Mattie) Ann Baggett (1869-1947), were the parents of seven children: Homer, Walter, Lula (Fisher), John Henry, Hattie Anne (Tormey), Fred, and Thelma (Sargent). J. J. Bland moved to San Augustine County from Georgia with his parents in about 1882.
— Courtesy Louise Martin

The Good Hope Church of Christ, built between 1886 and 1888, once stood on the property of T. W. M. Baggett in a small community north of San Augustine on FM #3230 (presently known as the Bland Lake Community). It also served as a school. In the 1890s, Good Hope became known as "Bugtussle," a name that was developed by a group of boys who watched the tumble bugs struggle and tussle in order to roll away the dried manure left behind by the horses.

— Courtesy of Dr. J. M. and McXie Whitton Martin

The old city hotel in San Augustine.

— Courtesy of Hazel Bellestri; printed in *The Rambler*

Turn of the Century in East Texas

THE TWENTIETH CENTURY BROUGHT new life to San Augustine. With the growth of urban industry, San Augustine, like many other small towns, prospered. Gins, mills, stores, schools, and churches provided the county seat and her smaller communities with employment, education, and recreation.

During this time, there were approximately fifty to one hundred or more rural communities with schools and churches in San Augustine County. Most people, mainly farmers, lived and worked in the rural communities without having to travel into San Augustine proper for supplies or work. A person was not only identified by his name, but also by the community in which he lived.

Most communities even had their own postal service and post office. One such community was Bland Lake, or "Stop," as it once was called. Beginning in 1903, Stop began its postal service with James J. Bland serving as postmaster. Other postmasters at Stop included Arthur Cottingham, John C. Hasley, Joseph C. Jones, and Bobbie Richards. Like most community post offices, postal service in Stop was discontinued in the 1950s.

The railway was a popular mode of transportation for people and goods. It was the only mode of transportation other than the horse and buggy, or automobile, if you were wealthy enough to own one. Often, San Augustine families would ride the railway to visit friends and relatives in other small cities such as Center or Nacogdoches.

Anne Miller Wharton remembers her grandparents saying that all of the materials of their house, including the framework and windows, were shipped to San Augustine via the railroad. Each part was numbered so the builders would know exactly where each part went during the home's construction.

Julia Howard Wade once said that her mother-in-law, Ara Atheniar Wade, often traveled on train from San Augustine to Carthage to visit relatives. On one particular visit, Mrs. Atheniar Wade, at that time a single young woman, decided she would accompany her cousin to an exam her cousin was taking to become a school teacher. Mrs. Wade wound up taking the exam also and passed with flying colors. Upon her return to San Augustine, Mrs. Atheniar Wade promptly quit school and began teaching at Steepcreek School.

Even though people boasted about the good life of San Augustine, the little town had its share of problems as well. During the early 1900s, most people knew San Augustine as the place of the Border and Wall feud. Most of San Augustine's citizens took shelter and kept their children out of harm's way in town because of this ongoing feud. George Wall, a son to Buck Wall, was sheriff when a young man named Kurg Border shot and killed him. It was not uncommon for the sheriff and his deputies to be at risk when it came to putting away criminals. The feud eventually ended with the ironic twist of Kurg Border becoming sheriff.

Almost every decade, an individual citizen would become a favorite son of San Augustine. For the first thirty years after the turn of the century, the Rev. George L. Crocket was the most well-known man in San Augustine. George L. Crocket was ordained an Episcopalian minister and served as rector of the Christ Church for nearly forty years. He was well-educated and also served as a professor of history at Stephen F. Austin State University in Nacogdoches. Crocket's most famous piece of work was the book *Two Centuries in East Texas.* This prolific book is still used today as one of the most accurate and well-documented sources of San Augustine history. No other author has attempted to present the history of East Texas and San Augustine as Crocket did. And thanks to Crocket's artistic abilities as well, historians today have a glimpse of what homes, businesses, and the town of San Augustine looked like in its early beginnings.

Crocket once wrote: "The art of the historian consists, not only in depicting the scene and action of past events; but also and more particularly in placing before us in his pages, the men and women who participated in these events, and by whose personality they were shaped. . . . As we look upon the mute buildings, changed perhaps beyond recognition by their former owners, . . . the imagination is able to repeople the scene with the form and presence of those who made the history that we can only write."

The mode of transportation during the latter part of the 1800s and the turn of the century.
— Courtesy of Agnes Williams Sparks

The dugout on Lobonella Creek, which was a popular hangout for young people in the early 1900s.
— Courtesy of Agnes Williams Sparks

*The Bland-Fisher home was built by James Jefferson Bland in 1912. It was the home of Federal Judge Joe J. Fisher and is currently owned by John Fisher. J.J. Bland was a lumberman, cornmeal miller, and ginner. *Historical Medallion Home*
— Patsy Jones

Corinth Primitive Baptist Church was organized in 1904 and is located in the White Rock community.
— Charla Jones

The James Benjamin Whitton home, built in 1903 for Whitton and his family by E.W. Weiderman and J.A. Clark. Whitton, his wife Ida Baggett Whitton, and their eight children lived here. Standing in front of the home were, from left, Hattie Whitton Winston, Lillis Whitton Anderson, Ben Whitton, Sue Smith, Irene Whitton Bickley, William Whitton, Jess Whitton, Julian Whitton, Abbie Whitton, and Nugent Whitton, who was killed in WWI. Those are visitors on the balcony.

— Courtesy of Dr. J. M. and McXie Whitton Martin

The Calvin and Margaret Hopkins Waley family. Seated are Forest, Calvin Waley, Pearl (Gill Van), and Margaret Waley. Standing in the background are Ethel (Whitton) and Leonard. Born later was their son, Garlan. Calvin Waley moved to San Augustine County in 1901 with his father, Michel Waley.

— Courtesy of Dr. J. M. and McXie Whitton Martin

Jim Langford and Ann Beasley Langford.

— Courtesy of Sandra Bennett

John and Ella Haley and their children.
— Courtesy of Sandra Bennett

Lela Ann Langford Fountain and Robert Elvin Fountain.
— Courtesy of Sandra Bennett

The Tinsley family, left to right front row: Genie Tinsley, Mary Tinsley, Ludia Tinsley, and Vivian Newton. Second row includes Minie Tinsley, Analiza Bland Tinsley, John W. Tinsley, Laura Tinsley Newton, and Robert Tinsley. Standing in the last row are Julia Tinsley, Silas Tinsley, unknown, and Robert L. Tinsley.
— Courtesy of Alvin Newton

The Robert L. and Laura Tinsley Newton family, c. 1917. They include, front row left to right: Ray Philmon, William Pete Newton, R.L. Newton, Pauline McEachern, Ruth Newton, Laura Tinsley Newton, and Mary Newton. The second row includes Dewey Newton, Vivian Newton Philmon, Sally Newton Neal, Frank Newton, Terry Philmon, Jessie Philmon, Earl McEachern, and Robert Newton. The back row is Chester Newton, Tom Chumley, Alberta Newton Chumley, Louise Chumley, Genie Newton McEachern, and W.F. McEachern.

— Couresty of Alvin Newton

Mary Elizabeth Dwire Campbell, maternal grandmother of Charla Jones and mother of Pasty Campbell Jones, when she was a young woman working in a retail store in San Augustine.

— Courtesy of the E. W. Campbell family

E.W. Campbell, husband of Mary Dwire Campbell, father of Pasty Campbell Jones and grandfather of Charla Jones, logging in the woods of San Augustine County.

— Courtesy of the E. W. Campbell family

Ernest R. Sparks with his son, Beeman, in the corn field.
— Courtesy of Agnes Williams Sparks

At left, George Tinsley delivers the mail to his father, John W. Tinsley, Agnes W. Sparks' great-grandfather.
— Courtesy of Agnes Williams Sparks

These are sergeants of the Sergeants Battery "F: 64th Arty. Cac." as numbered: 1: Weeks, Nacogdoches; 2: Smith, Nacogdoches; 3: Fauset, Med. Sgt. from Pittsburgh, PA.; 4: Meador, Nacogdoches; 5: Mast, Nacogdoches; 6: Mettauer, Chireno; 7: Muller, Nacogdoches; 8: Cordell, Garrison; 9: Rawls, San Augustine; 10: Reese, Nacogdoches; 11: Adair, Beeville; 12: Mentzel, Galveston; 13: Thodes, Beeville; 14: Perkins, Nacogdoches; 15: Herold, Sgt. Major from Cleveland, OH.; 16: Davidson, Nacogdoches; and 17: Hess, Texas City.
— Stephen F. Austin State University, East Texas Research Center

Amazon Dwire Ogden, the daughter of John and Cynthia Leach Dwire and the mother of Cynthia Ogden Martin. "Aunt Ammie" was a sister to Benjamin F. Dwire, maternal great-grandfather of Charla Jones and grandfather of Patsy Campbell Jones.
— Courtesy of the E. W. Campbell family

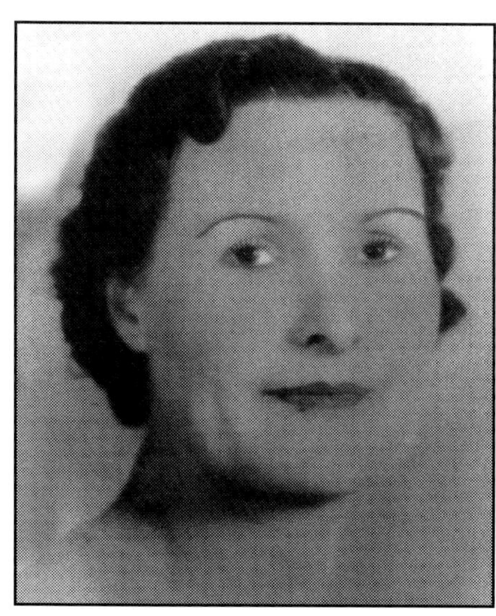

Audra Ford Sparks, wife of Ernest Richard Sparks.
— Courtesy of Agnes Williams Sparks

San Augustine Grammar School around 1928 or 1929, when the class of 1945 was in the second grade.
— Courtesy of Agnes Williams Sparks

Granberry School District No. 17 in San Augustine County, about 1909 or 1910. This was a community get together at Thanksgiving. The teachers were Tom Wall, Louis Wood, Sr., E.L. Perry, and Pearl Travis. From left to right on the front row are Minnie Wall, Edna Wall, Pearl Wall, Gladys Branberry, Maggie Jackson, Spurlock child, Edgar Pate, Link Wall, Bessie Perry, and Emma Spurlock. Second row includes Susan Spurlock, Allie Mae Wall, Fred Lee, August Jackson, Gradon Spurlock, George Wall, Walter Perry, Claud Lee, Bewley Byrd, and Oscar Jackson. The last row includes Norman Wall, Cleveland Wordsworth, Jeff Spurlock, Allen Travis, Rolan Perry, Giles Perry, "Buster" Spurlock, and Arthur Perry.
— Courtesy of R. N. Stripling Family

Goat Hill School.

— Courtesy of Agnes Williams Sparks

Blackjack School. Mary Knight Alvis, sister to W.K. (Bud) Knight, was the teacher. Lillie Mae Knight Williams is on the back row, third from left, and Maud Knight Williams is on the third row, third from left.

— Courtesy of Agnes Williams Sparks

Benjamin Franklin Dwire, grandfather and great-grandfather to Patsy Campbell Jones and Charla Jones, respectively, with his second wife, Miss Emma. They had two children of their own, Lois Dwire Cooper and Roxie Dwire Cash.

— Courtesy of the E. W. Campell family

Seated in their buggies from left to right are Aaron Coleman, Juanice Harvey Beard's grandfather, Mason, and Walter. They were about one-half mile from Broaddus near the Green home, c. 1916.

— Courtesy of Juanice Harvey Beard

Ace Clark, father of T. C. Clark.

— Courtesy of T. C. and Rose Clark

Bessty Holman.

— Courtesy of T. C and Rose Clark

Aaron and L. V. Wade Coleman, maternal grandparents of Juanice Harvey Beard.

— Courtesy of Juanice Harvey Beard

Gabriel Harvey and Sarah Burton Wood Harvey, seated, with their children Hilda, Ruthie, and Lillie. Standing to the left is the teacher, Georgie Galberry, who boarded with the Harveys, c. 1902. Gabriel was Juanice Harvey Beard's grandfather and a Church of Christ minister.

— Courtesy of Juanice Harvey Beard

Sulpher Springs school, approximately four miles southwest of Broaddus.

— Courtesy of Juanice Harvey Beard

Broaddus Depot, c. 1920.

— Courtesy of Nelda Allbritton Bell

Ruthie, Lillie, and Elvin Harvey in front of the Eli Harvey house, c. 1916.

— Courtesy of Juanice Harvey Beard

Leona and Mae Allbritton, aunts of Nelda Allbritton Bell, in front of the Broaddus school around fall 1929.

— Courtesy of Nelda Allbritton Bell

Brett Allbritton and friend, c. 1920.

— Courtesy of Nelda Allbritton Bell

Downtown Broaddus, c. 1912. Barnes Laurence is in the car. Woods-Taylor & Co. General Merchandise is the background. George Townsend's store, with the house behind it, was previously owned by Charlie Walton.

— Courtesy of Nelda Allbritton Bell

Hester Coleman, Juanice Harvey Beard's mother, on her horse, c. 1923.

— Courtesy of Juanice Harvey Beard

Mary Ann Mundine Beard, c. 1902.

— Courtesy of M. A. (Doc) and Juanice Harvey Beard

Jessie Layton Mundine and Rebecca Dikes, Doc Beard's maternal grandparents. Their two children are Mary Ann Mundine Beard (in front) and Marisella.

— Courtesy of M. A. (Doc) and Juanice Harvey Beard

Henry Sublett's father, Phillip William, with his two grandchildren, from left: Joe Phil Linear and David Mangan.

— Courtesy of Jane Mitchell Sublett

Benjamin A. and Ellen Chipman Beard, c. 1900. They were the paternal grand parents of M.A. (Doc) Beard.

— Courtesy of M. A. (Doc) and Juanice Harvey Beard

Betty Wood Oglesbee's grandfather, William Price Wood (at right) in front of his store where Nelsyn's is now located. His uncle A.J. Wood started the store. William Price Wood was married to Bettie Dixon Lewis Wood around 1906.

— Courtesy of John and Betty Wood Oglesbee

Inside the store of William Price Wood (at right). Notice the hat boxes at top right.

— Courtesy of John and Betty Wood Oglesbee

Bettie Dixon Lewis Wood dressed for a parade. She was the paternal grandmother of Betty Wood Oglesbee. This picture was taken where the City Lake is now located.
— Courtesy of John and Betty Wood Oglesbee

Raiford Nichols Stripling and Winfrey Leak Stripling. They married in 1909. Their children were Raiford Leak, Robert E., Frances, Sarah, Martha, and Mary Jane.
— Courtesy of the R. N. Stripling family

Lula Burkhalter, a telephone operator in San Augustine.
— Courtesy of the R. N. Stripling family

Eleanor Blonm, a former music teacher in San Augustine.
— Courtesy of the R. N. Stripling family

An interior shot of the Christ Church in 1901. Except for a few changes, the interior still looks much the same today.
— Stephen F. Austin State University, East Texas Research Center

Workers in the first telegraph office in San Augustine.
— Courtesy of the Citizens of San Augustine

The Red Cross Parade in downtown San Augustine, c. 1919.
— Courtesy of the Citizens of San Augustine

A view of the town. The Stripling-Tett's' drugstore is in background.
— Courtesy of the Citizens of San Augustine

A group of loggers with their team of horses taking logs to the local train station.
— Courtesy of the E. W. Campbell family

Edith Thompson, great-grandmother of Belinda Taylor Coulter, with her husband, Byron Lee Ware.
— Courtesy of Belinda Taylor Coulter

Judge William Charles Ramsey. He served as judge of the First Judicial District and as county judge. He and Emma Jenkins Ramsey were the parents of C.S. and Ben Ramsey and Lurette Ramsey Mitchell, mother of John and Charles Mitchell.
— Courtesy of C. S. Ramsey

Ratcliff school in 1907: 1. Vern Woodlam 2. Edd Woodlam 3. Jack Garrett 4. Earl Childers 5. Willie Garrett 6. Edward Rawson 7. Bart Woodlam 8. Ida Thacker Moss Goodwin 9. Maud Lee (Burks) 10. Ruth Moss (m. Fisher Rawson) 11. Vivian Garrett 12. Alma Pearl Butler 13. Bessie Kenner 14. Ennis Moss 15. Otis Sanders 16. Dumpsie Garrett 17. Inez Butler 18. J.W. (Bud) Butler 19. Delaney Woodlam 20. Sammie Sanders 21. Milton Garrett 22. Willie Woodlam 23. Levie Sanders 24. Floyd Sanders 25. Lester Rawson 26. Hub Butler 27. Gerald Rawson 28. Eugene Rawson 29. Earl Kenner

— Courtesy of Rosine Sanders Rawson

Denning school from left to right, first row: Mildred Rawson, Beatrice Hamby, Ruth Rawson, Gladys Nichols, Effie Dudley. Second row includes Audrey Sanders, Alanar Dudley, Felicia Watson, Cora Love, Arma Fitzgerald, Wilma Freeman. The back row includes Florence Rawson, Evie Butler, Coat Smith (cap on), Doll Bradberry, Rosine Sanders Rawson, Beatrice Bradberry, Ollie Nichols, ______, Gertrude Bradberry, ______, and Ora Gill.

— Courtesy of Rosine Sanders Rawson

Lelon, Hebert, and Rosine Sanders. Rosine married Lester Rawson.

— Courtesy of Rosine Sanders Rawson

W.C. Sanders and Etheal Harrell Sanders' wedding picture, December 14, 1902. They were the parents of Lelon, Rosine Sanders Rawson, Herbert, McNeil, Wayne, Lillian, Lester, Chester, Ruth, and Betty Sanders Elwell.

— Courtesy of Rosine Sanders Rawson

Columbus Lee Whitton. Lee was the father of Harlowe Whitton Johnson, Allene Whitton Hankla, and Rosa Whitton Ambrose.

— Courtesy of Rosa Lee Whitton Ambrose

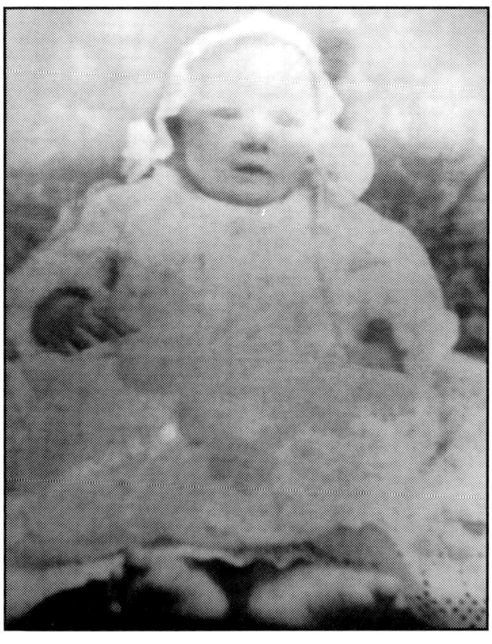

Mamie Ruth Ware Taylor as a baby. Miss Taylor is the grandmother of Belinda Taylor Coulter.

— Courtesy of Mamie Ware Taylor

The Jake Epps home just past the Antioch Church of Christ. The two unidentified people are sitting on an antique road grader.

— Courtesy of Alvin Newton

The Tinsley family and their musical instruments, from left to right: Robert Tinsley, Melvin Tinsley, Bessie Tinsley Flournoy, Evie Tinsley McSwain, Alice Bridges Tinsley, and Lawrence Tinsley.

— Courtesy of Alvin Newton

First Bland Lake schoolhouse, c. 1910. This picture was taken in 1912.Sallie Richards Whitton is on the second row, sixth from the left. Watsy Harris was the teacher.

— Courtesy of Sallie Richards Whitton

John E. and Minta Jones at their 50th wedding anniversary in 1950. They had nine children, one of whom was Mamie Ruth Patterson.

— Courtesy of Mamie Ruth Patterson

Lois Porcher Lewis and her twin brother, Lewis Porcher, on their 21st birthday. Lois was Anne Miller Wharton's maternal grandmother.

— Courtesy of Anne Miller Wharton

Lois Porcher Lewis (left) and her mother, Margaret Isabell Smith Porcher.

— Courtesy of Anne Miller Wharton

Rosie Harper (right), Rose Clark's grandmother, and Lizzie Lane.

— Courtesy of T.C. and Rose Clark

Theola Porter and friend by the railroad track in Broaddus.
— Courtesy of Marlon and Brownie Joe Minton

John Wesley Tinsley and his wife, Elizabeth Ann Bland Tinsley, a sister of J. J. Bland.
— Courtesy of Alvin Newton

Lee Whitton's daughters, from left to right: Harlowe, Allene, Mildred, and Rosa in front.
— Courtesy of Rosa Whitton Ambrose

The store which the Whittons owned. Jesse Whitton is to the left. It was located just below the site where the J. P. Mathew's store is today.
— Courtesy of Sallie Richards Whitton

W. H. Richards, Sallie Richards Whitton's father, at the syrup mill in Bland Lake.
— Courtesy of Sallie Richards Whitton

Gathering tobacco, c. 1917.
— Courtesy of Sallie Richards Whitton

Rose Clark's stepfather, Frank Mathews (1890-1993).
— Courtesy of T. C. and Rose Clark

Era Hagler is the only identified person in this photo. She is wearing white.
— Courtesy of Marlon and Brownie Joe Minton

Above and at left: The busy town of San Augustine.
— Courtesy of the R. N. Stripling family

Milton Wilkinson's grandfather, James Gipson Wilkinson (right), and a friend of his in Medford, Oregon, c. 1927. James Wilkinson came to Texas at the age of five and married Josephine Malone. He was a blacksmith and owned a country store a mile from the Hawthorne community.
— Courtesy of Dr. Milton Wilkinson

Teel and Hanks cotton yard.
— Courtesy of the R.N. Stripling family

The Cartwright home as it looked in the early 1900s.
— Courtesy of Anna V. Cartwright

The San Augustine High School in 1913.
— Courtesy of the R.N. Stripling family

The J. J. Bewley residence.
— Courtesy of the R. N. Stripling family

Several of the young ladies of San Augustine in the early 1900s. Mrs. Tom Blount is standing second from the left and Mrs. R.N. Stripling is standing fourth from the right.
— Courtesy of the R. N. Stripling family

Mr. R. N. Stripling loved to give candy to the ladies, according to his daughter Mary Jane Stripling. Here he is with some of his admirers.

— Courtesy of the R.N. Stripling family

An interior view of the Moss Hotel in 1906-1907. Seated at the lobby desk is W.S. (Dad) Moss. When the Mosses came to San Augustine in 1906, they purchased the building and established it as a hotel.

— Courtesy of the Citizens of San Augustine

Some San Augustine citizens standing in front of a downtown store, c. 1926.

— Courtesy of the San Augustine Public Library

The Rev. George Crocket standing behind his pulpit.

— Courtesy of Stephen F. Austin State University, East Texas Research Center

A hamburger stand on the courthouse square, c. 1915. Standing at left is Lem Henry and W.S. (Dad) Moss. Knight Parker once said they were the best hamburgers he had ever eaten. They were advertised as "made from the fruit of the hen," or in other words an egg was used in the making of the burger.

— Courtesy of Jerry Payne

Hugh Lawson Gamble and Mariah Josephine McCauley Gamble with their four oldest children, Tom, Martha, Minnie, and Maude c. 1900.
— Courtesy of Verline Gamble Stewart

The Garner Funeral Home, which started in 1926.
— Charla Jones

Hawthorne school, north of San Augustine in the Hawthorne community.
— Courtesy of the Citizens of San Augustine

The Clark-Downs store operated by Herman and Exa Doggett Clark in San Augustine.
— Courtesy of the Citizens of San Augustine

The courthouse in the 1920s.
— Courtesy of San Augustine Public Library

John Matthew Cartwright and his wife, Emily, the parents of Baxter Polk Cartwright, Sr.
— Courtesy of Anna V. Cartwright

Standing outside of Partin's Horses, Mules, and Cattle barn are W. R. Partin, Sr., Dallas Smith, and Brent (Sweet) McCoy.
— Courtesy of John and Betty Wood Oglesbee

The Gamble sisters: Minnie, Martha, and Maude, c. 1915. They were born in the Harmony community and are the great-granddaughters of James McCauley, who had a land grant from the Republic of Texas.
— Courtesy of Verline Gamble Stewart

Georgia Mae Woods Mathews' mother, Cora, with her eldest daughters.
— Courtesy of Georgia Mae Woods Mathews

Sam Houston Gamble riding a mule, c. 1928.
— Courtesy of Verline Gamble Stewart

Laura Cornelia Watson Fountain and Johnny Jackson Fountain.
— Courtesy of Sandra Bennett

Johnny Miller, paternal grandfather of Anne Miller Wharton.
— Courtesy of Anne Miller Wharton

Shug McKinney with his team of mules, pulling a wagon of logs. He was married to Consula Dwire and they had two children, Virgie McKinney Fort and Wade McKinney.

— Courtesy of the E. W. Campbell family

Kurg Border, former sheriff of San Augustine County.

— Courtesy of the R. N. Stripling family

A picture of the San Augustine courthouse in 1917, the year the flag was made by Ethel Beyer, wife of P. H. Beyer.

— Courtesy of San Augustine Public Library

A picture of San Augustine as it appeared in the early days.
— Courtesy of San Augustine Public Library

From left to right are Grizely Horton, Jim Thacker, Commissioner Bill Watson, and two unknowns.
— Courtesy of R. N. Stripling family

Looking down Columbia Street with Clark-Downs store at the right.
— Courtesy of San Augustine Public Library

One of San Augustine's busy streets in the early 1900s.
— Courtesy of San Augustine Public Library

A woman standing on the steps of First United Methodist Church long before concrete sidewalks.
— Courtesy of San Augustine Public Library

Patriotism Challenged

TIMES WERE TIGHT FOR EVERYONE in the U.S. during the 1930s and 1940s. The Great Depression and World War II had serious effects on small towns like San Augustine, causing people to lose a home or even worse a loved one in some distant battlefield.

Job Corps became popular during this time, especially for families who were having trouble making ends meet. Several of San Augustine's citizens lived and worked in Civilian Conservation Corps (CCC) camps in various parts of East Texas. Camps were located at Patroon and Milam; one of the African-American camps was at Bogota. These camps, involving mostly forestry work, were forerunners of the National Forestry Service.

The Work Projects Administration (WPA) was also a popular means of governmental work. The construction of schools, such as the San Augustine High School and other buildings, were constructed by this program. These buildings were made mostly from native rock, which distinguishes them from other types of building materials.

As in years past, the country was drawn in a war and the U.S. called for its people to stand against adversaries like Hitler just as Texas had defended itself against Santa Anna more than one hundred years before. Most of the young men in San Augustine joined the war effort. Patriotism was strong, but it wasn't the only reason young people enlisted; the Great Depression still lingered, and enlisting in the service provided a way for a young man to make a little money for himself and his family. Dr. Ira Brake was one of many San Augustine citizens who participated in the war, serving as a surgeon in North Africa.

Even though the main fighting took place in Europe and the Pacific, San Augustine saw the enemy up close without having to leave Texas. POW camps housing German prisoners were set up in East Texas, including San Augustine. Camp San Augustine was located across from San Augustine High School. George Goetz, a German who came to the U.S. as a teenager, served as a translator in the U.S. Army at Camp San Augustine. He later served as a state representative for approximately a year.

At the conclusion of the war, San Augustine experienced a "baby boom" experience as the rest of the nation did. As these youngsters grew into teenagers, the rural schools became overcrowded and, with a lack of funds, were unable to remain open. However, since transportation had been greatly improved, busing students from around the county into San Augustine proper was not a problem. African-American students attended Lincoln Colored High School, which was located on what was called Sunset or Ironosa Street.

School was important, but so was having fun. It was not unusual for groups of teenagers to invade Tom's Place or Bland Lake for a day of fun and relaxation. Tom's Place, owned by Tom and Irene Bickley, was located on Columbia Street just west of the square. This was a gathering place where teenagers could eat a burger, listen to music, and meet with friends. Dances, picnics, and swimming parties were popular at Bland Lake, a recreational facility during the summer months when school was out.

Often the famous and infamous came to San Augustine at the invitation of Claxton and Sarah Tucker Benedum, who owned Fairway Farm Hunt and Golf Resort. Anyone who played golf or had an interest in golf knew about Fairway Farm. Most golfers looked forward to playing on the excellent course designed by Claxton Benedum himself, and they enjoyed the companionship of Sarah Benedum who, in her own right, was a top-notch golfer. She had won several women's tournaments, including the club championship at the Shreveport Country Club. She was a descendant of Elisha Roberts of San Augustine and the daughter of Frank W. Tucker.

Mrs. Benedum said she once walked into the Broadmoor Country Club and in front of her a sign listed the top three golf courses in the U.S. of the 1960s. The foremost was Augusta in Georgia, the second was Cherry Hills, and the third was Fairway Farm in San Augustine. She was astounded because she did not know that Fairway Farm was so popular at that time.

San Augustine would produce another favorite son just as she had done many times before. In the 1940s and beyond, a young man, Raiford Stripling, developed into a well-known restoration architect, restoring many of Texas' famous historical landmarks. It was not uncommon to see Mr. Stripling and his driver, one of whom was Claudie Lane, driving down the road to a restoration job. Some of Stripling's work included restoration of the Mission Espiritu Santo at Goliad, the Independence Hall at Washington-on-the-Brazos, plus the Stephen W. Blount, Ezekiel Cullen, and Matthew Cartwright homes in San Augustine. During his latter years, Stripling lived in and restored the log home of Milton Garrett on Highway 21 west of San Augustine. His restoration efforts have left for generations to come a view of Texas' oldest historical landmarks as they appeared when they were originally built. Stripling, a graduate of Texas A&M, made his headquarters in the old San Augustine jail house.

It would happen that Claxton Benedum and Raiford Stripling would become very good friends. Sarah Tucker Benedum and Raiford Stripling had been childhood friends, and since Claxton Benedum sometimes asked for architectural advice, it seemed only natural that the Benedums and Striplings would be friends. Both Benedum and Stripling had a love for music and often Sarah would leave the two of them, along with other musician friends, to play all night at the clubhouse. Benedum played the guitar and Stripling played the bass fiddle.

Law and politics has been a part of San Augustine for a very long time. Many local citizens represented San Augustine in Austin, Washington, D.C., and internationally. Ben Ramsey served as lieutenant governor of Texas from 1951 to 1961. He also served on the Railroad Commission from 1961 to 1976. Edward A. Clark was chosen as the U.S. Ambassador to Australia in the 1960s. He and his wife, Anne, lived and worked in Australia many years before returning to Stradlefork. Anne Clark wrote a letter to her daughter, Leila, in 1965 regarding their first trip to Australia: "We arrived in Australia early Sunday morning, after spending two nights in Admiral Sharp's guest house in Hawaii. Admiral U.S. G. Sharp, Commander in Chief in the Pacific, is a direct descendant of General U. S. Grant. We also spent one night in Nadi Fiji. The time changes took a terrible toll on me. We lost a whole day; luckily it was Friday the thirteenth. I was not overwhelmed by the beauty of Hawaii as I had expected to be. The Rio Grande Valley has almost the same flowers and tropical verdure; it just lacks the blue Pacific and the mountains."

A sketch drawn by Mrs. Henry McLemore of Dr. Henry McLemore's grandfather's mill (P. S. McLemore) on the Patroon Road in the vicinty of where Dr. McLemore's office is now located.

— Courtesy of Dr. Henry McLemore

The East Texas high school champion baseball team from San Augustine, c. 1938. Team members in no certain order were G. W. Wood, Hugh Sparks, Jack Maund, LeRoy Sparks, Guy Stewart, Gene Partin, Jelly Coulter, H. T. Ware, J. L. Mathews, and O. J. Coulter.

— Courtesy of Agnes Williams Sparks

The sons of William Washington and Mary Lydia Hughes Whitton, left to right, are Lee, Jeff, Andrew, Ben, and Newt Whitton.

— Courtesy of Dr. J. M. and McXie Whitton Martin

The children of Beeman Sparks, Cornelia and Richard, c. 1949.

— Courtesy of Agnes Williams Sparks

Leon Rudd, LeRoy Sparks, and Hugh Sparks on Dutch Island near Aruba, c. 1943.
— Courtesy of Agnes Williams Sparks

Dr. Grover Stukey, a former doctor in San Augustine and friend to Agnes and LeRoy Sparks.
— Courtesy of Agnes Williams Sparks

The Home Life Insurance Co., with Ernest R. Sparks and his daughter Marie Sparks Roberts taking care of office business.
— Courtesy of Agnes Williams Sparks

Marie Sparks Roberts and her husband, Wyman Roberts. They owned the Wyman Roberts Funeral Home in San Augustine for many years.
— Courtesy of Agnes Williams Sparks

San Augustine class of 1945, front row left to right: Bobbie Lou Noble, Kathryn Hanks, Rosa Nell Smith, Marie Isenblitter, Betty Jean Sparks, Myrtle Walton, Frances Murphy, Betty Merle Sanders, Myrtle Young, Bobbie Louise Cunningham, Lucille Higginbotham, Rena Jean Blackstock, Mae Yvonne Reeves, Allyne Sowell, and Alice Louise Thompson. Second row includes Brooksie Kennemer (Sponsor), Agnes Williams Sparks, Delores Tannery, DuVergne Birdwell, Mary Beth Allen, June Norvell, Joy Holt, Betty Jo Murphy, Laverne Conn, Liberene Hanks, Helen White, Brooksie Butler, Mary Lee Sheffield, Jewel Lynch, Willie Sue Eppes, Mozelle Williams, Dorothy Mae Tannery, Maxine Stockman, Maurine Ponder, Billy Anders, Bruce Goldman (Sponsor). Back row includes Jack Arnold, Richard Murphy, Irion Bate, Corkey Eppes, Harold Birdwell, Herbert Wood, Laurie "Boo" Mathews, Nelwyn Carter, Kenneth Halbert, Charles Wither, Pat Henry Fussell, Haven Evett, and Lynn Lister.

— Courtesy of Agnes Williams Sparks

T.C. Clark and his brother, Edward Clark, c. 1948.
— Courtesy of T. C. and Rose Clark

Elsa V. "Doll" Hart was a teacher at Lincoln Colored High School in San Augustine.
— Courtesy of T. C. and Rose Clark

Standing at left is F. D. McClure and at right James Teel. McClure was the principal at Lincoln Colored High School and Teel was Sunday school superintendent at Reed Chapel.
— Courtesy of T. C. and Rose Clark

The Rev. R. L. Taylor (left), former pastor of Reed Chapel, and the Rev. A. L. Patterson, former husband of Mamie Patterson and former pastor at Lanetown.
— Courtesy of T. C. and Rose Clark

John R. Johnson (1901-1985), Rose Clark's father.
— Courtesy of T.C. and Rose Clark

T. C. Clark and Miller Mathews.
— Courtesy of T.C. and Rose Clark

Edward Matthews (1936-1959), son of Frank Matthews (1890-1993).
— Courtesy of T. C. and Rose Clark

Horace Bryant, a former teacher at Lincoln Colored High School and nephew of Rose Clark.
— Courtesy of T. C. and Rose Clark

Broaddus school, c. 1930.
— Courtesy of Juanice Harvey Beard

Sam and Mary Beard, M. A. (Doc) Beard's parents, c. 1947.
— Courtesy of M. A (Doc) and Juanice Harvey Beard

A portrait of Federal Judge Joe Fisher.
— Stephen F. Austin State University,
East Texas Research Center

Juanice Harvey Beard and her brother, Wondale Harvey, in front of the old syrup mill, four miles southwest of Broaddus, c. 1930.
— Courtesy of Juanice Harvey Beard

Mance Mitchell on his horse. Mance Mitchell was married to Julia Jones Mitchell and they were the parents of Jane Mitchell Sublett.
— Courtesy of Jane Mitchell Sublett

Doc Beard's father and his siblings. Left to right: James McKinney Beard, Susie Ellen Beard Allbritton, ?, Cordy Beard Craver, Sam Cephas Beard, George Tom Beard, Dora Annie Beard Tisdale, and Dorcey Crockett Beard.
— Courtesy of M. A. (Doc) and Juanice Harvey Beard

McXie Day Whitton, a former teacher.
— Courtesy of the R. N. Stripling family

The Stripling daughters aligned according to age, starting at left: Frances, Sarah, Martha, and Mary Jane.
— Courtesy of the R.N. Stripling family

The SFA Board of Regents at Dr. Ralph Steen's inauguration in Nacogdoches. From left to right are Dr. Steen, William V. Brown, Henry Sears, C.S. Ramsey (San Augustine), Hubert Mills, Elizabeth Koch, Jack Woodward, Richard Stovall, and Frank White. (The name of one of the four from the far right is missing).

— Stephen F. Austin State University, East Texas Research Center

Former state representative George Goetz (left) and former U.S. Senator Ralph Yarborough in 1957.

— Stephen F. Austin State University, East Texas Research Center

A young First Sergeant George Goetz (in jeep) and an unidentified G.I. at Camp San Augustine during 1944. Goetz served in the U.S. Army as a translator at Camp San Augustine. The brick home in the background belonged to the Keidels.

— Stephen F. Austin State University, East Texas Research Center

Sheriff Hoyt Marshall, c. 1940s.
—Courtesy of Citizens of San Augustine

Swimmers enjoying a day at Bland Lake, c. 1940s.
— Courtesy of Citizens of San Augustine

San Augustine Grammar School.
— Courtesy of Citizens of San Augustine

The old Hampton Hotel in San Augustine.
— Courtesy of the Citizens of San Augustine

Cecil Murphy, former county clerk and father to Richard and Neal Murphy.
— Courtesy of Richard Murphy

A young Arlan Hays doing what he loves best, working on the newspaper. His father was owner and editor of the San Augustine Tribune.

— Courtesy of Citizens of San Augustine

Dr. Ira Fyke Brake came to San Augustine in 1935 and served as a physician and surgeon until his death in 1952. He served in the U.S. Army Medical Corps in North Africa and southern Europe during WWII.

— Courtesy of Mrs. C.S. Ramsey

C. S. (Smith) Ramsey joined his father in 1928 in the practice of law and in operating the San Augustine County Abstract Company. C. S. Ramsey remained active in the firm until the time of his death in 1983. He served as city attorney for about forty years. In 1957, he was appointed by Governor Allan Shivers to a six-year term on the Board of Regents for State Teachers Colleges.

— Courtesy of Mrs. C. S. Ramsey

Ben Ramsey served as lieutenant governor of Texas and railroad commissioner. Ramsey and William P. Hobby (left) held the office of lieutenant governor longer than anyone else, respectively. Ramsey joined his father and brother in their law firm and the San Augustine Abstract Company sometime after 1928. Ramsey also served as secretary of state (1949-1950), state senator (1941-1949), and state representative.

— Courtesy of Dr. C. R. and Mary Jean Haley

Herman Clark was a brother to the former ambassador to Australia, Edward Clark. Their parents were David and Lelia Downs Clark.

— Courtesy of Exa Doggett Clark

Exa Doggett Clark was married to Herman Clark. They ran the Clark-Downs store for many years until 1932. She has been the Rotary Club sweetheart since 1970.

— Courtesy of Exa Doggett Clark

McNeil Sanders, son of W. C. and Etheal Harral Sanders, was the San Augustine County treasurer for over forty years. He was the father of Carol Wayne Vaughn.

— Courtesy of Rosine Sanders Rawson

Rose Clark as a 1946 senior.
— Courtesy of T. C. and Rose Clark

Mamie McCoy Johnson, Rose Clark's mother.
— Courtesy of T. C. and Rose Clark

Richard McCoy, an uncle to Rose Clark.
— Courtesy of T. C. and Rose Clark

Inside Miller's Cleaners, owned by Johnny Miller, Anne Miller Wharton's grandfather.
— Courtesy of Anne Miller Wharton

Margaret Lewis Miller with son, Lewis Nolen Miller, Anne's father.
— Courtesy of Anne Miller Wharton

Mildred Whitton Smith, sister to Harlowe Whitton Johnson, Allene Whitton Hankla, and Rosa Whitton Ambrose.
— Courtesy of Rosa Whitton Ambrose

The senior class at Camp Worth, c. 1938-39. From left to right are Lessie Sims, Buster Fountain, J.T. Holt, Max Fuller, and Janie McSwain.

— Courtesy of Harlowe Whitton Johnson

San Augustine teachers Wilma Polley and Harlowe Whitton Johnson (right).

— Courtesy of Harlowe Whitton Johnson

Lee Whitton's 90th birthday celebration with his daughters, Harlowe, Allene, and Rosa.

— Courtesy of Harlowe Whitton Johnson

The Johnson twins, Elfrieda Rogers (left) and Juanita Simmons (right).

— Courtesy of Harlowe Whitton Johnson

Camp Worth teachers, from left to right: Gertrude Powers, LaNell Still, Pauline Frederick, Marie Kirk, and Harlowe Johnson.

— Courtesy of Harlowe Whitton Johnson

Camp Worth students, from left to right: Temple Lee Fountain, Ardella Fountain, John Fountain, Faye Cody, Elton McSwain, and twins Era and Veva Martin.

— Courtesy of Harlowe Whitton Johnson

Harlowe Johnson (front), James Dennis, Robert Caston, and Dr. D. E. Bailey after they had all won a school board election.

— Courtesy of Harlowe Whitton Johnson

Samuel L. and Millie Frances Willard family gathering.

— Courtesy of Harlowe Whitton Johnson

First Baptist ladies social at the home of Mr. and Mrs. W.M. Wade, c. 1941. First row, left to right: Mary Ponder, Mollie Richey, Annie Brittain, ______, Weedie Wilkinson, and Mrs. J.P. Owen. Second row includes Mrs. Wall, Julia Harvey Crocker, Mrs. Josie Whitton, and Maggie Rhodes (Nelsyn Wade's grandmother). Third row includes Eunice Roberts, Bettie Bierhalter, Della Armstrong, Mrs. Sanders, Lena Fussell, and Esta Price.

— Courtesy of Nelsyn and Julia Wade

Anna Kathryn Rulfs Holbrook, a former English teacher at San Augustine.

— Courtesy of Harlowe Whitton Johnson

Gertrude Johnson Lane, c. 1946, her first year in college.

— Courtesy of William and Gertrude Johnson Lane

From left to right: Barfield Burrows, Mrs. W. M. Wade, Jean Marie Mason, Eunice Lee Ponder, Garland Burrows, Lucille Whitehurst, and Laurence D. Rulfs.

— Courtesy of Nelsyn and Julia Wade

Front row, seated left to right: Avis Smith, Mrs. Fred Thompson, Margaret Wade, and Mary E. Saunders. Standing left to right: Mary Carlyn Thomas, Minnie T. Butts, Melba Nooner, Mrs. Carl Thomas, Hallie Pearce, June Goen, Lucille Whitehurst, Mrs. Rudy Maude Knoll, Exa Crouch Carroll, Florence Eddings, and Lila Smith.

— Courtesy of Nelsyn and Julia Wade

Jim Fireship, who worked for the railroad.
— Courtesy of Marlon and Brownie Joe Minton

Inside the Wades' cafe from left to right are Steve Crumpler, Mrs. W. M. Wade, Vela Crumpler, Price, and Pearl Fox.
— Courtesy of Nelsyn and Julia Wade

Eugene Marlon Minton, Jr., son of Eugene, Sr. and Mary Minton, and Milton Wilkinson, son of the Rev. Eugene and Letha Wilkinson, 1953, on the day they recieved their master's degrees from Stephen F. Austin State University in 1953. Minton is married to Brownie Joe Campbell Minton, sister of Pasty Campbell Jones and aunt of Charla Jones.
— Courtesy of Marlon and Brownie Joe Minton

Mrs. W. M Wade's family, from left to right: Emily Rhodes Carter, Ettie Lee Rhodes Tubbe, Magdalene Nations Rhodes, Arthur Rhodes, and Ara Atheniar Rhodes Wade, mother of Nelsyn Wade.
— Courtesy of Nelsyn and Julia Wade

Seated from left to right: Pauline McDaniel, Mrs. Paul Wright, Della Hines, and Christine Mathews. Second row includes Mrs. Tom Blount, Inga Hays, Frances Sparks Weaver, Betty Jean Sparks Cartwright, Francis Woods, Mrs. R. N. Stripling, Nealy Jane Stevenson, and Exa McEachern.

— Courtesy of Nelsyn and Julia Wade

Charlie Mills, former mail carrier.

— Courtesy of Nelsyn and Julia Wade

Mrs. Tom Blount, Mrs. R. N. Stripling, and Julia Wade at a social function at the Cullen House.

— Courtesy of Nelsyn and Julia Wade

Some of San Augustine's citizens outside of the Wade Cafe.
— Courtesy of Nelsyn and Julia Wade

The Deep East Texas Electric Cooperative when it was first built in San Augustine.
— Courtesy of the Deep East Texas Electric Cooperative

The linemen and their trucks, Deep East Texas Electric Cooperative.
— Courtesy of the Deep East Texas Electric Cooperative

Tom and Annie T. Burris Blount in front of their home, which is now the office of Dr. John Oglesbee III.
— Courtesy of the R. N. Stripling family

The Brewer family from left to right, seated, Wiley Brewer and Alice Slagle Brewer. Standing are their children, Juanita Brewer Noble, Liz Ware's father Bill Brewer, Ethel Brewer Howard, George Brewer, and Pauline Brewer Walton.
— Courtesy of Leeon and Liz Ware

Lon Ware, father of Leeon Ware, at his saw mill. The other man is Frank Collins.

— Courtesy of Leeon and Liz Ware

Dr. John Henry Ellington practiced medicine in Patroon and San Augustine. He was married to Verna Bell Ellington from Patroon and they had one child, Alice Joy Ellington Weaver. He obtained his medical degree in 1901.

— Courtesy of Alice Joy Ellington Weaver

Dr. Charles Haley, father of Dr. C. R. Haley, in his medical office in Bastrop, LA. Dr. Haley came to San Augustine as a physician after obtaining his medical degree from Vanderbilt University and teaching medicine at Tulane Medical School.

— Courtesy of Dr. C. R. and Mary Jean Haley

Milton Wilkinson and his son, Nick, meet President Harry Truman. Milton and his wife, Bonnie Hope Wilkinson, traveled the world as Goodwill Ambassadors during President Johnson's administration.

— Courtesy of Dr. Milton Wilkinson

Milton Wilkinson's mother, Letha Mae Mitchell Wilkinson, and her cousin, Rudy Mitchell, father of John and Charles Mitchell, in their later years.

— Courtesy of Dr. Milton Wilkinson

Anna V. and Baxter Polk Cartwright, Sr., the parents of Baxter Polk Cartwright, Jr. and John Matthew Cartwright. Anna was born in the Old Union community to Walter Theophilus and Susan Temperance Roberts. Anna is a former school teacher.

— Courtesy of Anna V. Cartwright

Several of San Augustine's citizens dressed in 1800s attire for the 1936 centennial celebration.

— Courtesy of the R. N. Stripling family

San Augustine High School class of 1934-35.

— Courtesy of Class of 1935

The children of Monroe Ponder in the Hebron community, c. 1935. From left to right are Chester Ponder, Harley Dodson, Orin Ponder, Benard Ponder, Kathryn Ponder, Calvin Ponder, and Burl Thornton, a first cousin.
— Courtesy of Jim and Winnie Ponder Nance

Jackie Estes Gamble holding her twin daughters, Verline Gamble Stewart (left) and Merline Gamble, c. 1936.
— Courtesy of Verline Gamble Stewart

Sam Houston Gamble, c. 1930.
— Courtesy of Verline Gamble Stewart

Noble and Co. From left to right: Harry P. Noble, Sr., O. H. Irwin, Willard Folsom, Homer Murray, Billy Richardson, George Neal, Doyle Graham, Carmen Fussell, J. W. Parker, Harry P. Noble, Jr., Franklin Bush, Charles Newberry, Carl Ponder, T. H. White, Cleatus Sowell, Jack Sowell, and Johnnie Runnels.

— Courtesy of the San Augustine Public Library

The Highway Department, c. 1950s. From left to right: Elray Baggett, Jim Arnold, Huey P. Long, Hally McKinzey, Willie Holt, Bill Henley, Oran Davis, Thomas Baggett, Johnny Ray Norwood, Hollis Stringer, Archie Lynch, Ralph Colemen, Alvin Newton, Pete Murphy, Oran Jones, and Tray Hayes.

— Courtesy of Alvin Newton

R. N. Stripling behind the counter in his drugstore.
— Courtesy of the R. N. Stripling family

The White Rock school building in the White Rock community.
— Charla Jones

From left to right are Dr. Tipps, Dr. Curtis Haley, James Green, Dr. J. M. Buchele, and Dr. N. T. Bennett.
— Courtesy of Dr. C. R. and Mary Jean Haley

Cynthia Ogden Martin, daughter of Amazon and Ola Ogden and mother of Irenus and Beeman Martin. Cynthia worked at the Pentagon in Washington, D.C. during the Kennedy administration.
— Courtesy of the E. W. Campbell family

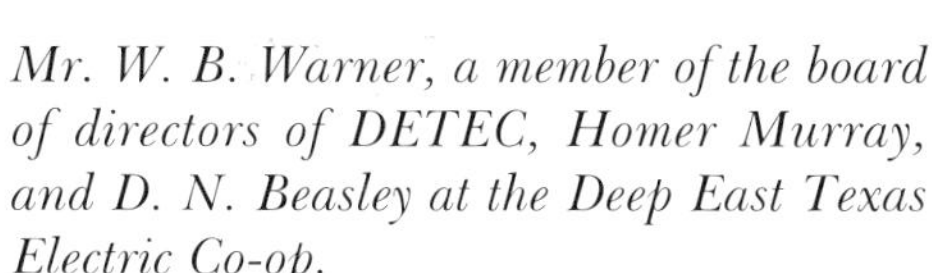

Mr. W. B. Warner, a member of the board of directors of DETEC, Homer Murray, and D. N. Beasley at the Deep East Texas Electric Co-op.
— Courtesy of the Deep East Texas Electric Cooperative

Mr. W. B. Warner and Mr. Raiford L. Stripling, father of Raggy Stripling.

— Courtesy of the Deep East Texas Electric Cooperative

McXie Whitton Martin, Irene Whitton Bickley, and Miriam Whitton Nations stand in front of Tom's Place, a popular hangout for young people from 1939 to 1956. It was built by Tom and Irene Bickley. Tom's Place also had carhops and music for kids to dance to. Seated in the background, Lovedy Bickley.

— Courtesy of Dr. J. M. and McXie Whitton Martin

The sons of Ben and Ida Baggett Whitton, left to right: Jesse, Julian, Abbie, and William, with their father, Ben Whitton, c. 1938. William Whitton was McXie Whitton Martin's father.

— Courtesy of Dr. J. M. and McXie Whitton Martin

The old jail house which became the office of architect Raiford Stripling and later the office of his son, Raggy Stripling.
— Charla Jones

The Dairy Mart in the 1950s.
— Courtesy of Jerry Payne

Tony Ball and an unidentified soldier at Camp San Augustine in the 1940s.
— Stephen F. Austin State University, East Texas Research Center

Raiford Leak Stripling, the famous architect of San Augustine, at work. Stripling was the son of R. N. and Winfrey Leak Stripling and the father of Raggy Stripling. He graduated from Texas A&M and is famous for his restorations of historical landmarks in Texas, including the mission at Goliad, Washington-on-the-Brazos, and the Blount, Cullen, Milton Garrett, and Columbus Cartwright homes in San Augustine.
— Courtesy of Ray R. Stripling

The Rev. Eugene and Letha Mae Mitchell Wilkinson, the parents of Dr. Milton Wilkinson.
— Courtesy of Dr. Milton Wilkinson

One of San Augustine High School's senior classes.

— Courtesy of Dr. C. R. and Mary Jean Haley

The hotel committee at the opening of the Holiday Inn. Seated from left are Mrs. Butts, Mrs. Matthew Buchele, Mrs. J. H. Oglesbee, Julia Howard Wade, and Betty Wood Oglesbee. Standing left to right are Dr. J. M. Buchele, Mr. J. H. Oglesbee, Sr., Mr. Nelsyn Wade, and Mr. John Oglesbee, Jr.

— Courtesy of John and Betty Wood Oglesbee

Edward Clark, second from left, and members of his family.
— Courtesy of Leila Clark Wynn

The Queen's Court, spring 1939. From left to right in the front seated are McXie Whitton Martin, John Harvey Butts, Bobby Perry, and Miriam Whitton Nations. Second row seated are Kenneth Stephenson, Sue Caldwell Simmons, and Sue Butts McEachern; standing is Arthur Smith, Jr. On the third row, Henry Sublett, Johnnie Taylor King, (the Queen) Ann Hall King, (the King) Edward Thomson, Jr., Gene Bishop, Wilma Berry Woods. Standing on the back row are Hugh Sparks, Kathleen Cobb Menkin, Hollis Eppes, and Lois Butler Bailes.
— Courtesy of Dr. J. M. and McXie Whitton Martin

Children in the Harmony community, c. 1942. From left to right are Merline Gamble, Hugh Oscar Gamble, Verline Gamble Stewart, Jimmie Jean Skipper, Dorothy Sharpton, Shirley Skipper, and Maxie Skipper.
— Courtesy of Verline Gamble Stewart

Students of the Harmony school at a birthday party, c. 1945. Front row left to right are birthday boy Walter Martin, Georgia Kennon, and Willie Lowery. Second row are Jerry Kennon, Jimmie Skipper, Shirley Skipper, Merline Gamble, Verline Gamble Stewart, E.C. Kennon, James Perry, and Thomas Gamble. Back row includes Maxie Skipper, Dorothy Sharpton, Bobby Sharpton, Herman Kennon, and Hugh Oscar Gamble.
— Courtesy of Verline Gamble Stewart

In front of the Chevrolet garage c. 1940s. Kneeling from left to right are T.J. Woods, Sonny Sublett, Pete Newton, and Brice Jones. Standing from left to right are Archie Birdwell, Jake Bradberry, Dan Sublett, Quary Jasper, and Oscar Birdwell.
— Courtesy of Alvin Newton

Cora Woods was elected Homecoming Queen at a San Augustine school reunion. Mrs. Woods was in her nineties at the time.
— Courtesy of Georgia Mae Woods Mathews

Mary Ann and Ed Horn.
— Courtesy of Alvin Newton

The San Augustine County courthouse as it appears today with the statue of the first governor of Texas, James P. Henderson.

— Courtesy of Charla Jones

A group of men gathered in front of the Morriss and Hudson Livestock barn in San Augustine, c. 1939.

— Courtesy of Citizens of San Augustine

This photo is of a group of students who attended Camp Worth school in the 1930s.

— Courtesy of Harlowe Whitton Johnson

Photo taken at the Wade home at a gathering hosted by Mrs. Wade. She is seated on the front row at the far right.
— Courtesy of Nelsyn and Julia Howard Wade

M. A. (Doc) Beard, c. 1930s, standing in front of the home where he was born in Broaddus.
— Courtesy M. A. (Doc) and Juanice Harvey Beard

Federal Judge Joe Fisher speaking before an audience while Mary Jean and Curtis Haley look on.
— Courtesy of Dr. C. R. and Mary Jean Haley

The Quality Flower and Beauty Shop which once stood on the east side of the courthouse square. Hazel Bellestri owned the store.

— Courtesy of Hazel Bellestri

Former U.S. Ambassador to Australia Edward Clark.

— Courtesy of Dr. C. R. and Mary Jean

Former President Lyndon Johnson shaking hands with his friend, former Ambassador to Australia Edward Clark.

— Courtesy of Leila Clark Wynn

Seymour Thomas, a famous artist from San Augustine. He was married to Helen Haskell. He died in 1956 at the age of eighty-eight. He was the grandson of Stephen W. and Mary Landon Lacy Blount and son of James Edward and Mary Landon Blount Thomas. This is a self-portrait of Thomas.

— Courtesy Ezekiel Cullen House and Museum, San Augustine

Dr. Ira Brake, looking like a 1930s movie star. Dr. Brake was a surgeon in San Augustine for many years.

— Courtesy of Harlowe Whitton Johnson

John Connally, Ben Ramsey, and a young Charlie Wilson.
— Stephen F. Austin State University, East Texas Research Center

Standing in the middle is former Ambassador to Australia Edward Clark and his daughter, Leila Clark Wynn. (At left, unidentified.)
— Courtesy of Leila Clark Wynn

San Augustine Restored

THE TRADITIONS OF SAN AUGUSTINE from its early beginnings have been kept alive by its successive generations. Many of the historical homes still belong to the descendants of families who originally owned them. These new generations maintain the old homes and preserve the history of the towns.

Of the businesses and organizations that began years ago, most have been updated to better serve the San Augustine area. The Deep East Texas Electric Co-op is today one of the best rural electrical businesses in Texas. Its past and present board members have worked to ensure that San Augustine and a large part of East Texas stay "well lit."

San Augustine still receives its news from a source which has seen most of the town's history since the turn of the century. Arlan Hays continues as publisher of the *San Augustine Tribune* today. His father, Webster F. Hays, bought the paper in 1916. Arlan began working at the paper when he was eight years old, eventually becoming publisher in 1934. The *Tribune* had been the first newspaper of Galveston, but it was moved to San Augustine in 1837. In the 1890s, a young lady of sixteen took the money she made from two bales of cotton on the two acres her daddy had given her and bought the San Augustine newspaper. She did not want her brother, a printer, to lose his job.

Some believe that San Augustine had the first boy scout troop in Texas since it was named Troop #1. It has been said that George L. Crocket attended a scout meeting in Galveston. When he returned to San Augustine, he organized a boy scout troop in the city and it was called Troop #1, with Crocket as the scoutmaster. Many young men have worked and participated in the troop's scouting activities. In 1989, San Augustine had eleven young men achieve the status of Eagle Scouts, a most unusual feat. The Eagle Scouts were Forrest Oglesbee, Jason Ellis, Cade Downs, Eric Goodwin, Charles Goodwin, Dexter Richards, William Holverson, John Raymond Johnson, Scott Castle, John Fussell, and Greg Sherman. John Oglesbee, Jr., was the scoutmaster.

San Augustine has another group of young people in training, but this training comes in the form of preserving history for future historians. The Junior Historians is an organization that seeks to promote the continuation of preserving the history of San Augustine. As the oldest Anglo-Saxon county in Texas, and boasting several favorite sons and daughters, there is a lot of history to preserve for the generations to come.

In future years, two more historical sites will be added to San Augustine. A historical museum created by the San Augustine County Historical Foundation is under construction. This museum, which is located in the old movie theater on Columbia Street, will house artifacts, art, period costumes, and photographs commemorating the history of San Augustine. It will also be a performing arts theater for local civic and school clubs.

There are also plans to construct a museum to commemorate the Mission Nuestra Señora de los Dolores de los Ais. This facility will be located along the banks of the Ayish Bayou on Highway 147, approximately the same location of the original mission. Archaeologists for years have been excavating the area for artifacts. The project should be completed within the next few years.

Often, the upkeep of historical sites is quite exhausting. The George L. Crocket home, which recently burned, will hopefully be restored in the coming years by the San Augustine County Historical Foundation. It was located on Market Street across from Christ Church Episcopal.

As George L. Crocket once wrote concerning *Two Centuries in East Texas,* his first intention was to write a brief story of San Augustine, but as his research progressed his brief story turned into three hundred pages. There is almost too much history in San Augustine, but having grown wiser as she has grown older, the town has quite a lot to say to future generations about her past and how understanding that past can lead to a better future.

Highway 21, or the King's Highway, today looking from the Louisiana side toward Texas.

— Charla Jones

The King's Highway today now crosses Toledo Bend, which was built in the 1960s along the Sabine River. The majority of emigrants crossed this very place hundreds of years ago.

— Charla Jones

San Augustine Public Library, which was once the Iona Hotel. The library is one of the best in East Texas, containing hundreds of books and documents on genealogy and historical facts of San Augustine.

— Charla Jones

The J. J. Bewley residence was a turn of the century home built atop a hill on South Liberty Street. Today David and Frances Sparks Maxwell own the home.

— Charla Jones

The Wade Home, built in the 1940s for Mr. and Mrs. Wade. Nelsyn, the Wades' son, and his wife, Julia, have turned the home into a bed and breakfast.

— Charla Jones

The clubhouse at Fairway Farm from the eighteenth green. Claxton Benedum designed the clubhouse himself; he and his wife, Sarah Tucker Benedum, a descendant of Elisha Roberts and daughter of Frank W. Tucker, built Fairway Farm Hunt and Golf Resort on Highway 21 east of San Augustine.

— Charla Jones

The Honorable Gertrude Lane, who is currently mayor of San Augustine. She is the first African-American woman and the second woman to hold the position of mayor.

— Courtesy of Gertrude Johnson Lane

Chapel Hill Methodist Church on Highway 21 east of San Augustine near the Ford's Corner community.

— Patsy Jones

An old store in the Ford's Corner community east of San Augustine on the King's Highway.

— Charla Jones

The front left room of the Ezekiel Cullen Home as it appears today. The Cullen House and Museum was restored by Raiford Stripling.

— Patsy Jones

Upstairs in the Cullen Home, where dances were formerly held, are artifacts from historical San Augustine. This mannequin is dressed in a formal funeral attire for a widow who would have worn such a dress in the 1800s.

— Charla Jones

The current Chamber of Commerce office and tourist center in San Augustine. It is reminiscent of a log cabin. The Chamber building sits on the bank of the Ayish Bayou.

— Charla Jones

A view of the back of the Chamber of Commerce building shows the seven flags which flew over San Augustine: Spain, Mexico, France, the Fredonians, the Republic of Texas, the Confederate flag, and the U. S. flag.

— Charla Jones

The Cartwright home on South Liberty as it appears today. The house remains much the same as it did when it was built in the early 1900s. The exception is the porch, which once extended around the second floor.

— Charla Jones

A shoreline view of City Lake just south of San Augustine proper.

— Charla Jones

The old movie theater on Columbia Street has been renovated into a historical museum by the San Augustine County Historical Foundation. This museum will house artifacts and photographs of historical San Augustine and will serve as an auditorium for various programs in the city.

— Charla Jones

San Augustine High School, which still stands today on Hwy. 147 N. The rock building and wall were built by the WPA in the 1930s.

— Charla Jones

Arlan Hays, age eighty-two, still sees that San Augustine is kept up-to-date with the news in the San Augustine Tribune. *Mr. Hays' father was the publisher of the* Tribune *for years, and Mr. Hays has carried on that tradition.*

— Charla Jones

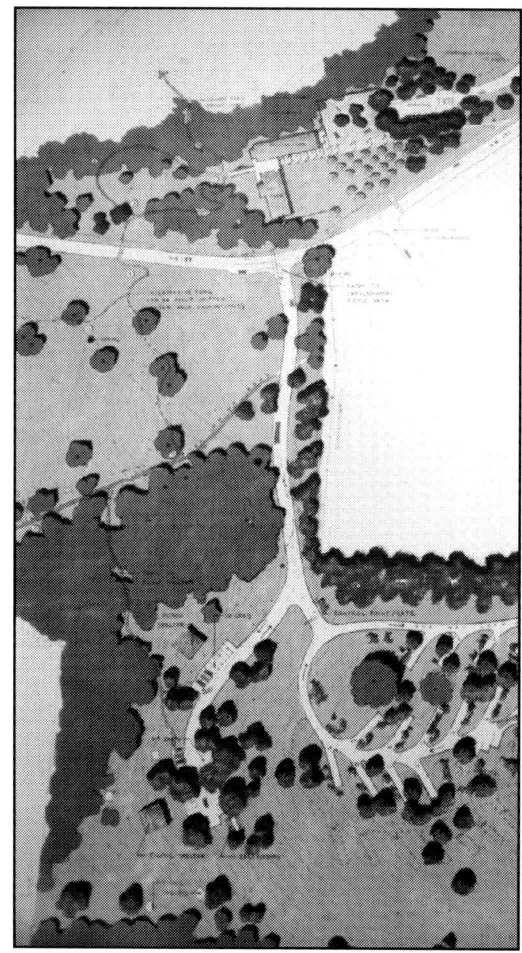

An aerial view of the proposed mission museum site on Highway 147 near the Ayish Bayou, where the Mission Nuestra Señora de los Dolores de los Ais once stood. The museum is located at the top of the picture and the R V campsite is located at the bottom.

— Charla Jones

A model of the City of San Augustine MissionNuestra Señora de los Dolores de los Ais Visitors and Interpretive Center. At the bottom right will be a courtyard leading into the museum. The building will house a visitors center, a laboratory for identification of artifacts, and a reading room.

— Charla Jones

The former home of Tom and Annie T. Burris Blount, now the office of Dr. John H. Oglesbee III on Hospital Street.
— Charla Jones

A spectacular marker for the graves of Columbus Cartwright and his wife, Sallie. The graves are in the San Augustine City Cemetery.
— Charla Jones

The San Augustine City Cemetery, where many of San Augustine's heroes and dignitaries are buried.
— Charla Jones

The former bus station in San Augustine, now the office of Dr. C. R. Haley on Main Street.
— Charla Jones

The former home of Capt. L. D. Downs. It was once a bed and breakfast, but today it is the home of Mr. and Mrs. Pat Fussell.
— Patsy Jones

The former home of John Mason Rankin. It burned in 1909 and was rebuilt by Rankin's daughter Fannie, a former teacher in San Augustine. Today the home is owned by Harry and Jean Noble.

— Patsy Jones

The Red Land Lodge #3, the third lodge founded in the state of Texas.

— Charla Jones

McMahon's Chapel east of San Augustine. Although the church is located in Sabine County, it is the oldest Protestant church in Texas; its founder, Littleton Fowler, also helped erect First United Methodist Church in San Augustine.

— Charla Jones

An inside view of McMahon's Chapel as it looks today.

— Charla Jones

A carved rock commemorating the early Methodist Circuit Riders and ministers who helped found McMahon's Chapel and the Methodist religion in Texas. The rock is located in the cemetery adjacent to McMahon's Chapel.

— Charla Jones

A view of Ayish Bayou, which runs through San Augustine. Brush and trees surround the bayou today, but it still manages to flood low-lying areas when it rains hard.

— Charla Jones

The 17th green at Fairway Farm Golf Course. The golf course and country club are no longer open.

— Charla Jones

Sarah Tucker Benedum and her husband, Claxton Benedum. They built and operated Fairway Farm on Highway 21 east of San Augustine during the 1950s and 1960s.

— Courtesy of Mrs. Sarah Benedum; printed in *The Houston Chronicle Magazine,* January 24, 1960

The altar in the Christ Church Episcopal. The altar was carved by its former rector, George L. Crocket. He also did other carvings symbolic of the church.

— Charla Jones

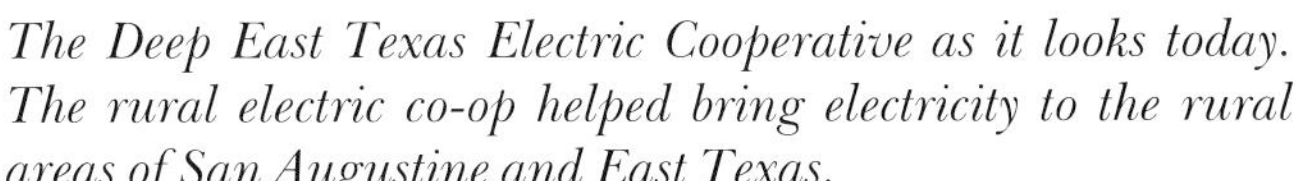

The Deep East Texas Electric Cooperative as it looks today. The rural electric co-op helped bring electricity to the rural areas of San Augustine and East Texas.

— Charla Jones

Notes

pg. xiii:

Spanish missionaries first came to East Texas: Crocket, G. *Two Centuries in East Texas,* chapters 1, 2, and 3.

The Aies, a tribe from . . . lived along the Ayish Bayou: Nardini, L. R. *No Man's Land*, pg. 3.

Spanish missionaries erected missions: Allen, C. & Clark, A. *Historical Homes of San Augustine*, pg. 3.

the missionaries apparently failed to truly convert. Crocket, G. *Two Centuries in East Texas,* chapters 1, 2, and 3.

San Augustine would be inhabited and vacated almost four times: Crocket, G. *Two Centuries in East Texas.*

Richard Sims arrived in 1792. . .: Crocket, G. *Two Centuries in East Texas,* pgs. 63, 64, 82, 83, and 84.

pg. xiv:

. . . possessed good educations. . . Crocket, G. *Two Centuries in East Texas,* pg. 78.

Numerous cotton gins and lumber mills. . .: Crocket, G. *Two Centuries in East Texas,* pgs. 88, 89.

. . . *The* Athens of Texas: Crocket, G. *Two Centuries in East Texas,* pg. 299.

One of the first known schools. . . : Crocket, G. *Two Centuries in East Texas,* pg. 330.

San Augustine was home to two universities: Crocket, G. *Two Centuries in East Texas,* pg. 300.

San Augustine University board of trustees: Crocket, G. *Two Centuries in East Texas,* pg. 301.

Fourteen citizens . . . served on board . . : Crocket, G. *Two Centuries in East Texas,* pg. 307.

. . . James P. Henderson and his partners. . . : Winchester, R. G. *James Pinckney Henderson.*

One of the requirements to own land. . . : Jones, C. *House Stands Testament of Time.* Texas magazine of *The Houston Chronicle,* February 18, 1996.

Houston was baptized a Catholic. . . : Jones, C. *House stands testament of time.* Texas magazine of *The Houston Chronicle,* February 18, 1996.

Alexander Horton fought in the Battle. . : Malone, S. (ed.) *Alexander Horton: Patriot of the Republic of Texas by Alexander Horton.*

Kenneth L. Anderson served. . . : Ramos, M. G. *Texas Almanac 1996-1997,* pg. 499.

Other men who served. . . : Crocket, G. *Two Centuries in East Texas,* various pages.

Frances Cox Henderson's role: Farrell, M. D. *First Ladies of Texas.* pgs. 64-75.

She was solely responsible. . . : Allen, C. & Clark, A. *Historical Homes of San Augustine.* pg. 44.

pg. xv:

Mrs. Henderson, who was educated. . . : Winchester, R. G. *James Pinckney Henderson,* pg. 49.

Antioch Church of Christ. . .: Driskill, F. A. & Grisham, N. *Historical Churches of Texas,.* pg. 83-85.

Goodlaw's Presbyterian. . . : Lynch, W. E. *The Cradle of Texas: Presbyterianism.*

McRae Church. . . : Allen, C. & Clark, A. *Historical Homes of San Augustine,* pgs. 28, 60.

The First United Methodist Church. . . : Cartwright, A. T., Dorsey, R. P., Rickey, B. P., with McDonald, A. P. *First United Methodist Church of San Augustine,* Tindall, W. E. *First United Methodist Church; San Augustine, Texas.*

. . . building the first Protestant church: Cartwright, A. T., Dorsey, R. P., Richey, B. P., with McDonald, A. P. *First United Methodist Church of San Augustine.* pg. 8.

pg. 1:

Ayish Bayou District: Crocket, G. *Two Centuries in East Texas,* pg. 85.

. . . hostility of the Western Indians. . . : Crocket, G. *Two Centuries in East Texas.*

Caddoes were main tribe. . . : Newcomb, W. W., Jr., *Indians of Texas.*

The Caddo nation was divided. . . : Nardini, L. R. *No Man's Land.* pg. 3

Other local tribes . . : Nardini, L. R. *No Man's Land,* **pg. 3.**

Dr. Donald E. Chipman: *The Daily Sentinel,* April 7, 1996. Heritage by Lucille Fain.

I came to this county. . . : Malone, S. (ed.) *Alexander Horton: Patriot of the Republic of Texas by Alexander Horton,* pg. 1.

pg. 2:

From 1806 until 1821. . . : Nardini, L. R. *No Man's Land,* pg. 87.

The area . . . called Free State. . . : Nardini, L. R. *No Man's Land,* pg. 87.

The first house built. . . : Malone, S. (ed.)*Alexander Horton: Patriot of the Republic of Texas by Alexander Horton,* pg. 18.

Horton was aide-de-camp to Houston: Malone, S. (ed.) *Alexander Horton: Patriot of the Republic of Texas by Alexander Horton.*

Mial Scurlock: Martin, E. W. *The Scurlocks: Seekers of Freedom*, pg. 107.

San Augustine lived under seven flags. . . : Interview with John Oglesbee, Jr.

pg. 16:

U. S. and President Polk. . . : Hogan, W. R. *The Texas Republic: A Social and Economic History*, pg. 5.

Jones stated. . . : Hogan, W. R. *The Texas Republic: A Social and Economic History*, pg. 5.

in the early 1840s. . . : Winchester, R. G. *James Pickney Henderson*, pgs. 50-51.

A story of Roberts Baptist Church. . . : Phillips, J. *Roberts Baptist Church, 100th Anniversary*.

. . . list of San Augustine's wealthiest. . . : *San Augustine Tribune*, October 26, 1995.

Sublett nominated Houston. . . : Interview with Harry P. Noble, Jr.; Allen, C. & Clark, A. *Historical Homes of San Augustine*, pg. 50.

James Pinckney Henderson: Winchester, R. G. *James Pickney Henderson*, pg. 10.

Had Anderson not died. . .: A synopsis: Texas State Library, Lorenzo de Zavala Archives and Library.

pg. 17:

[Henderson] practiced law. . . : A synopsis: Texas State Library, Lorenzo de Zavala Archives and Library.

Henderson filled the vacancy. . . Winchester, R. G. *James Pinckney Henderson*, pg. 98.

O. M. Roberts was another governor. . . : Ramos, M. G. (Ed). *Texas Almanac*. pg. 499.

made major improvements. . . : A synopsis: Texas State Library, Lorenzo de Zavala Archives and Library.

He helped found. . . : A synopsis: Texas State Library, Lorenzo de Zavala Archives and Library.

. . . he taught law. . . : A synopsis: Texas State Library, Lorenzo de Zavala Archives and Library.

Roberts made San Augustine famous. . . : Excerpts from lecture given at the University of Texas, May 26, 1893 by O. M. Roberts. Excerpts from Malone, S. (Ed.), *Alexander Horton: Patriot of the Republic of Texas by Alexander Horton*, pg. 70.

. . . Edwards once told. . . : Malone, S. (Ed.). *Alexander Horton: Patriot of the Republic of Texas by Alexander Horton*, pg. 73.

Marriage ceremony of Horton. . . : Smith, R. *The Life of Alexander Horton*, pgs. 218-219.

Nine of San Augustine's Confederate soldiers. . . : Driskill, F. A. & Grisham, N. *Historical Churches of Texas*, pg. 85.

Dr. Roberts served. . . : Crocket, G. *Two Centuries in East Texas*, pg. 343.

pg. 31:

Stop began a postal service. . . : Sanders, J. B. *San Augustine County, Texas 1850 Census*. Interview with Sallie Richards Whitton.

Postmasters for Stop: Sanders, J. B. *San Augustine County, Texas 1850 Census*. Interview with Sallie Richards Whitton.

Anne Miller Wharton remembers. . . : Interview with Anne Miller Wharton.

Julia Howard Wade recalls her mother-in-law. . . : Interview with Julia Howard Wade.

George Wall. . : *A Texas Sheriff*. Malone, S., printer, pgs. 35-43.

. . . feud ended. . . : *A Texas Sheriff*. Malone, S., printer, pgs. 35-43.

pg. 32:

George Crocket served as rector. . . : Allen, C. & Clark, A. *Historical Homes of San Augustine*, pgs. 34, 44.

pg. 60:

Dr. Ira Brake served in WW II. . . : Interview with Opal Ramsey.

Tom's Place: Interview with McXie Whitton Martin.

pg. 61:

Often the famous. . . : interview with Sarah Tucker Benedum.

Mrs. Benedum walked into Broadmoor. . . : Interview with Sarah Tucker Benedum.

Raiford Stripling: McCullar, M. *Restoring Texas: Raiford Stripling's Life and Architecture*.

. . . Stripling's work included. . . : McCullar, M. *Restoring Texas: Raiford Stripling's Life and Architecture*, pgs. 116, 119, 123, 126, and 128.

Benedum and Stripling friends. . . : McCullar, M. *Restoring Texas: Raiford Stripling's Life and Architecture*, pg. 67; Interview with Sarah Tucker Benedum.

Ben Ramsey: Ramos, M. G. (Ed.). *Texas Almanac*, pg. 500.

Anne Clark wrote to her daughter: Clark, A. *Australian Adventure: Letters from an Ambassador's Wife*.

pg. 96:

Arlan Hays' father bought. . . : Interview with Arlan Hays.

It has been said Crocket attended. . . : Interview with Arlan Hays.

San Augustine had eleven Eagle Scouts. . . : Interview with John Oglesbee, Jr.

A historical museum. . . : San Augustine County Historical Foundation meetings; Interview with John Oglesbee, Jr.

pg. 97:

mission tourist center: Interview with Alton Shaw.

. . . his first intention. . . : Crocket, G. *Two Centuries in East Texas*, preface.

Crocket house burned: *San Augustine Tribune*, May 16, 1996.

Bibliography

A Texas Sheriff (1987, 2nd reprint). S Malone, Printer: San Augustine, TX.

Allen, C. (editor) & Clark, A. (1972). *Historical Homes of San Augustine.* San Augustine Historical Society and Encino Press: Austin, TX.

Bolton, P. (1947). *Governors of Texas.* Texas Quality Newspaper.

Bracken, D. K. & Redway, M. W. (1956). *Early Texas Homes.* Southern Methodist University Press: Dallas, TX.

Brewer, Mattie Sharp, Papers. Stephen F. Austin State University, East Texas Research Center, Nacogdoches, TX.

Cartwright, A. T., Dorsey, R. P., Richey, B. P. with McDonald, A. P. (1976). *First United Methodist Church of San Augustine, TX 1837-1976.*

Clark, A. (1969). *Australian Adventure: Letters from an Ambassador's Wife.* University of Texas Press: Austin, London.

Class of 1945. (1995). *50th Reunion Commemorative Book.* Graphic Arts classes: San Augustine High School, Mike Malone instructor.

Combs, J. F. (1968). *Gunsmoke in the Redlands.* Naylor Co.: San Antonio, TX.

Crocket, G. (1932). *Two Centuries in East Texas.* Hart Graphics, Inc.: Austin, TX.

Crocket, George L. Papers. Stephen F. Austin State University, East Texas Research Center, Nacogdoches, TX.

The Daily Sentinel. The Herald Publishing Co., Nacogdoches, TX. Owned wholly by Cox Enterprises, Inc.

Driskill, F. A. & Grisham, N. (1980). *Historic Churches of Texas.* Eakin Press, Burnet, TX.

Ericson, C., Ericson, J., McDonald, A. P. & Partin, J. (1995). *Nacogdoches.* Best of East Texas Publishers: Lufkin, TX.

Farrell, M. D. (1976). *First Ladies of Texas.* Stillhouse Hollow Publishers: Belton, TX.

Henson, M. S. & Parmelee, D. (1993). *The Cartwrights of San Augustine.* Texas State Historical Association: Austin, TX.

Hill, J. M. (1935). *Heores of Texas.* Union National Bank: Houston, TX.

Hogan, W. R. (1946). *The Texas Republic: A Social and Economic History.* University of Oklahoma Press: Norman, OK.

Jones, C. R. (February 18, 1996). *Home Stands the Testament of Time.* Texas magazine, The Houston Chronicle: Houston, TX.

Lytch, W. E. (1993). *The Cradle of Texas: Presbyterianism.* Providence House Publishers: Franklin, TN.

Malone, S. (editor). (1984). *Alexander Horton: Patriot of the Republic of Texas by Alexander Horton.* S. Malone, Printer: San Augustine, TX.

Martin, E. W. (1985). *The Scurlocks: Seekers of Freedom.*

McCullar, M. (1985). *Restoring Texas: Raiford Stripling's Life and Architecture.* Texas A&M Press: College Station, TX.

McDonald, A. P. (1978). *Eastern Texas History: Selections from the East Texas Historical Journal.* Jenkins Publishing Co.: Austin, TX.

Nardini, L. R. (1961). *No Man's Land: A History of El Camino Real.* American Printing Co.: New Orleans, LA.

Newcomb, W. W., Jr. (1961). *The Indians of Texas.* University of Texas Press: Austin, TX.

Perttula, T. K. (1992). *The Caddo Nation.* University of Texas Press: Austin, TX.

Phillips, J. (1972). *Roberts Baptist Church, 100th Anniversary* San Augustine, TX.

Ramos, M. G. (editor). (1996). *Texas Almanac.* Dallas Morning News: Dallas, TX.

The Redlander. A. W. Canfield, publisher.

San Augustine Tribune. Arlan Hays, publisher. San Augustine, TX.

Sanders, J. B. (1965). *San Augustine County, Texas 1850 Census.* J. B. Sanders, 409 Nacogdoches Street, Center, TX.

Seale, W. (1949). *San Augustine in the Texas Republic.* Encino Press: Austin, TX.

Smith, R. (1936). *The Life of Alexander Horton.* Thesis presented to the University of Texas graduate faculty in 1936.

Texas Highways. Texas Department of Transportation: Austin, TX. Travel and Information Division.

Tindall, W. E. (1984 reprinted). *First United Methodist Church; San Augustine, Texas.* C. V. A. E.: San Augustine High School, Mike Malone instructor.

Wilson, Karle Baker, Papers. Stephen F. Austin State University, East Texas Research Center, Nacogdoches, TX.

Winchester, R. G. (1971). *James Pinckney Henderson.* Naylor Co.: San Antonio, TX.

Winegarten, R. (1993). *Governor Ann Richards and Other Texas Women.* Eakin Press: Austin, TX.

Woolworth, L. F. (1936). *Littleton Fowler: A Saint of the Saddle-Bags.* S. Malone, Printer: San Augustine, TX.

Index

Errata and Additional Notes by McXie Whitton Martin

PAGE XI *3rd paragraph:* **They found the land inhabited by the Caddo Indians** The Ais Indians were of the Hasinai Indians, a confederation of the Caddo, yet spoke a different language than the Caddo. It was from the Hasinai word friends of allies Texas got its name. (source: The Texas State Historical Association, *The New Texas Handbook,* Vol. I, 76, 1996; Dr. George Louis Crocket, *Two Centuries in East Texas,* 1932, 6.)

Along this bayou the Spanish missionaries erected missions if "this bayou refers to the above "Ayish Bayou" only one (1) mission was erected, "Mission Neustra Señora de los Dolores de los Ais", founded first in the spring of 1717, abandoned in 1719, fearing the French would attack as the results of the war between Spain and France in Europe." Rebuilt in August 24, 1721; (source: Donald E. Chipman, *Spanish Texas, 1519–1821,* Austin: University of Texas Press, 1992; *de la Pena, the diarist of the Aguayo expedition.*)

According to many sources, the missionaries apparently failed to truly convert all of the Indians to the Catholic religion, therefore causing the Spanish government to close the missions throughout East Texas (The reason the Spanish missions and presidios were erected in the first place was to lay their claim to Texas, and to keep the French in Louisiana from encroachment into Texas. From 1729 until 1772 Los Adais was the capital of Coahuila y Tejas. It is true the missionaries failed in their work but that was not the reason the missions closed. A year before the Treaty of Paris was signed in 1763, thus ending the Seven Year War in Europe (1754–1763), known as the French and Indian War in America, by a secret agreement France had ceded Louisiana to Spain. In 1772, San Antonio became the capital of Coahuila y Tejas, therefore the missions and presidios were no longer needed as a barrier against the French. In the summer of 1773, the East Texas missions were closed and all the Spanish settlers moved to San Antonio. (source: Donald E. Chipman, *Spanish Texas, 1519-1821,*University of Texas Press, 1992; Texas Historical Association, *The New Texas Handbook,* Vol. 5, pp.13, 20.)

Page XI, *4th paragraph:* **The Spaniards often traded goods with the Indians and with the French who had controlled Louisiana** (this took place prior to the next sentence.) **This made the town of San Augustine** (founded in 1833. Prior to this date, the area was known as the Ayish Bayou District. (source: legal documents, land deeds, and other records housed in the vaults located in San Augustine County Clerk's office, San Augustine Courthouse; R. B. Blake Collection, Stephen F. Austin University, Nacogdoches, Texas.)

Page XI, *5th paragraph:* **However, after Spain lost the Texas territory to Mexico,** (Mexico won their independence from Spain in 1821, after which Texas became a province of Mexico) **the Mission Nuestra Señora de los Dolores de los Ais was vacated** (this took place in 1773.)

Page XIII, *2nd paragraph:* **"The Antioch Church of Christ,** the oldest congregation in the State of Texas was organized in 1833 by Dr. William Defee in the home of Rodney Anthony. In 1836 the members constructed a log building on the Anthony property and continued meeting there until 1870 when they moved to the present site. In 1880, Stephen Passmore, Sr. deeded the property to the Elders of the church, T. W. M. Baggett and N. W. Ware, for the purpose of worship services and a school. The 1880 structure was replaced in 1938 with a "classic revival" building. (source: data on the Texas Historical Commission Marker located in front of the building; Stephen Daniel Eckstein, Jr. *History of the Churches of Christ in Texas,* Firm Foundation Publishing House, 1963; Texas Historical Association, *The New Texas Handbook,* Vol. 2, pp. 105-107. The Antioch Cemetery has a Texas Historical Commission Marker at the entrance.) {use this data for page 4}

Page XIII, *2nd paragraph:* The first organized **Old School Presbyterian Church in Texas** was organized by Hugh Wilson, June 2, 1838, in the Goodlaw School, four miles west of San Augustine. In 1840, the congregation moved into the town of San Augustine and changed the name from "Bethal Presbyterian" to "The San Augustine Presbyterian Church." When the present building was constructed in 1887, the name was changed to "Memorial Presbyterian Church." (source: data in part on the 1936 Texas Historical Marker; William E. Lytch, *The Cradle of Texas Presbyterianism, History of the Memorial Presbyterian Church,* Franklin, TN, Providence House Publishers, 1993; Texas Historical Association, *The New Texas Handbook* Vol. 5, 327.) {use this data for page 12}

The United Methodist Church was first organized as the Methodist Episcopal Church in the fall of 1837 by Littleton Fowler. The cornerstone was laid January 17, 1838. Angered when his horse was turned loose while in church, Columbus Cartwright in 1897 donated an entire block across the street for a new sanctuary, provided a post for hitching horses and space for parking buggies. The present United Methodist Church building was completed in 1911. As directed in the deed, there is a hitching post still standing in front of the building. (source: data in part from the State Historical Survey Committee Marker located on the Methodist Episcopal site and the Texas Historical Commission Marker located in front of the present United Methodist Church building; Texas Historical Association, *The New Texas Handbook,* Vol. 4, 645.)

McMahan's Chapel, the oldest Methodist church in the state of Texas, was organized in the home of Samuel McMahan in Sabine County by James P. Stevenson in September of 1833. Littleton Fowler, the full-time minister of the church, died in 1846, and at his request is buried under the pulpit. The present building (the fourth) was built in 1956. The historic McMahan cemetery is located to the east of the building. (source: Texas State Historical Association, *The New Handbook of Texas,* 1996, Vol. 4, 434.)

Page XIII, *4th paragraph:* **Today, San Augustine boasts more than twenty historic sites in the city and county.** (There are more than fifty (50).)

Page XIII, *last paragraph:* San Augustine is the oldest Anglo-Saxon town in the state of Texas, laid out in 1833 on the American plan.

Page 1, *2nd paragraph:* **Before the revolution, the Ayish Bayou District consisted of San Augustine, its surrounding area, and parts of Shelby County.** (In 1834 the Ayish Bayou District became the Municipality of San Augustine that included the present counties of San Augustine, Shelby, Sabine, and part of the counties of Panolo, Newton, and Jasper. In 1835 the Municipality of San Augustine only included the present county of San Augustine.

Page 1, *last paragraph, continued on page 2:* **The Neutral Strip (1806-1821) extended from Robeline, La. downward to the Sabine Lake and westward to Natchitoches in La. (Natchitoches is east of Robeline)** *The New Texas Handbook,* Vol. 4, 983, states in part: The Neutral Strip was never officially stated other than a general statement: The EAST boundary was the Arroyo Hondo, the same boundary line between Louisiana and Texas in 1736, it was a small stream between La Adaes and Natchitoches. The WEST boundary of the Neutral Strip was the Sabine River; it is assumed the NORTHERN boundary was the thirty-second parallel of latitude; and the SOUTHERN boundary was the Gulf of Mexico.

Page 4: The Antioch Church of Christ. Refer to correct data on page XIII, above.

Page 8, *top photograph:* **CHINA GROVE** is two (2) words.

Page 9, *top left photograph:* **The Wade House** was built in 1875. T. S. C. Wade moved to Texas in late 1846. (source: Nelson Wade.)

Page 11, *lower right photograph:* **The Ezekiel Cullen Home;** Texas Historical Medallion Home; it is also listed on the National Register.

Page 13, *top right photograph:* **The Matthew Cartwright Home;** Texas Historical Medallion Home; it is also listed on the National Register.

Page 13, *lower right photograph:* **Christ Episcopal Church** was organized in 1848, not in 1838. (source: History of Christ Episcopal Church)

Page 17, *6th paragraph:* Correct spelling of Alexander Horton's wife's surname: Harrell, not Harrol.

Page 18, *middle right photograph:* **The William Garrett Home;** Texas Historical Medallion Home; it is also listed on the National Register.

Page 19, *top left photograph:* **Methodist Church,** Refer to correct history on page XIII above.

Page 20, *middle left photograph:* **The Hollis building** was built in 1889 on the site of the Kenneth L. Anderson Law Office.

Page 29, *lower right photographs:* Courtesy of Louise Bland Martin.

Page 31, *last paragraph:* This is a time in history that is nor generally talked about in San Augustine. Most of us stay away from this issue out of respect to some families involved. It is part of our history. Mr. Joseph F. Combs did publish a book in 1968, *Gunsmoke in the Redlands.* I will give you a brief outline. The correct spelling of Kurg Border is Curg. The last sentence is incorrect, in part. The feud did not end when Curg became sheriff. Border killed Sheriff George Wall, April 21, 1900; charged September 12, 1900 in district criminal court; the trial was moved to Shelby County for obvious reasons; but dismissed in January of 1901, since his associates made sure there was no testimony against him; elected sheriff in November of 1902 by intimidation; in 1903 an organized group of citizens presented in District Court a petition charging Border with crimes while in office; Border was removed as sheriff March 2, 1904; killed May 7, 1904 when he, his sister Cora, and a friend tried to kill the newly elected sheriff.

Page 45, *lower right photograph:* Courtesy of *Mrs.* C. S. Ramsey. Mr. Ramsey is deceased.

Page 50, *middle left photograph:* The wife of John W. Tinsley was ANALIZA Bland Tinsley, a sister of J. J. Bland and HARRIETT BLAND BAGGETT.

Page 102, *top right photograph:* Refer to **McMahan's Chapel** data on page XIII.

Page 102, *middle left photograph:* **The Redland Masonic Lodge** was organized in 1837.